The Projective Use of Mother-and-Child Drawings

A MANUAL FOR CLINICIANS

The Projective Use of Mother-and-Child Drawings

A MANUAL FOR CLINICIANS

Jacquelyn Gillespie, Ph.D.

Routledge
Taylor & Francis Group
New York London

First published 1994 by BRUNNER/MAZEL, INC.

Published 2014 by Routledge

Routledge
Taylor & Francis Group
711 Third Avenue
New York, NY 10017

Routledge
Taylor & Francis Group
27 Church Road
Hove, East Sussex BN3 2FA

First issued in paperback 2015

Routledge is an imprint of the Taylor & Francis Group, an informa business

Library of Congress Cataloging-in-Publication Data

Gillespie, Jacquelyn.
The projective use of mother-and-child drawings : a manual for clinicians / Jacquelyn Gillespie.
p. cm.
Includes bibliographical references and index
ISBN 0-87630-736-5
1. Object relations (Psychoanalysis) 2. Mother and child. 3. Drawing—Psychological aspects. 4. Projective techniques. I. Title.
[DNLM: 1. Projective Techniques. 2. Mother–Child Relations. 3. Art. WM145 G478p 1994]
RC455.4.023G54 1994
616.89'17—dc20
DNLM/DLC
for Library of Congress 94-11439
CIP

ISBN 13: 978-1-138-88369-7 (pbk)
ISBN 13: 978-0-87630-736-6 (hbk)

Dedicated
for obvious reasons
to the memory of my mother

HAZEL M. HUNTER

and to my children

CATHERINE LAROCHE
THOMAS RANDALL GILLESPIE

and to my granddaughter

JACQUELYN LAROCHE

Contents

Foreword

Lawrence E. Hedges, Ph.D.

Depth Psychology has undergone a major shift in thought during recent years. And it is this paradigm shift which Dr. Gillespie's wonderful book so delightfully explores and graphically portrays.

Freud's self-analysis in 1897 demonstrates the ways in which unconscious thought may be considered. Freud maintains that unconscious primary-process thought can be witnessed in dreams, slips of the tongue, humor, and sexuality (1900, 1901, 1905). And, following Dr. Gillespie's text, we can now add artistic productions. Primary-process thinking was shown by Freud to operate on the basis of metaphor and metonymy—condensation and displacement—in contrast to the operation of the ordinary logic of conscious, secondary-process thinking.

Carl Jung, Alfred Adler, Wilhelm Reich, and many others incorporated Freud's "topographic" paradigm of the unconscious into their depth psychologies. By 1923 Freud clarified a paradigm shift that was occurring throughout the depth psychologies. This "structural" model for psychological investigation contrasts the person's developing sense of I (ego) with other aspects of the life force, the it (id). The investigative question regarding any given psychological state or complex then becomes: How is the agency of "I" experienced in relation to other aspects of the life forces that operate in a person? And, of course, Freud noted the perennial presence within the sense of I of sociocultural and linguistic influences, the over-I (superego). Depth psychological investigation thus came to include not only a consideration of conscious and unconscious thought, but also of the operative internal personality structures or agencies, the I, the it, and the over-I.

Carl Jung early in his investigations began to speak of the self as the center of the personality. But it was not until 1950 that Heinz Hartmann created for classical psychoanalysis and ego psychologists the conceptual distinction between the agency of ego as a set of personality functions and the self as the organizing center of the personality. Edith Jacobson is generally credited with formulating the foundations of what has become a major shift in thought. In *The Self and the Object World* (1964) Jacobson declares that when working with more depressed or more deeply disturbed people in analysis, Freud's topographic paradigm of the unconscious, and Freud's structural paradigm of id, ego, and superego simply do not help her. Jacobson reports that studying analytically the way in which a person represents self in relation to others gives her the analytic leverage required. That is, by studying with the person the ways in which their internal patternings of self and other representations are structured, it becomes possible to bring to consciousness those subjective constructions that govern a person's relations to the world. Thus "self and other" psychology has emerged to revolutionize the way depth psychology now investigates psyche. Gillespie's text makes a special addition to the ways psychologists have come to study self and other representations.

Four main watersheds or listening perspectives are now evident in an array of self and other representational possibilities. These four perspectives for psychotherapeutic investigation can be considered in terms of the mythic themes they evoke as well as their relation to studies in psychopathology. In order to fully contextualize Gillespie's present work it may be helpful to mention these perspectives briefly.

Historically, the first perspective for listening to self and other representations emerged from Freud's self-analysis as he discovered in his own dreams triadic relational themes reminiscent of Sophocles' *Oedipus Rex* and Shakespeare's *Hamlet*. Freud defined neurosis as a set of three-party emotional relatedness patterns learned by a child in the fourth through seventh years of life, but unnecessarily (i.e., neurotically) retained in later love relationships. The impulses toward incest and parricide that children this age brashly express and then learn to repress comprise an "Oedipus Complex," which persists in its unconscious influence on the person's love life. Heinz Kohut (1982) reminds us that Oedipus was given away at birth because of an oracle's predictions. Such rejection is bound to produce negativity in a child. By way of contrast, Kohut (1982) cites the mythic theme of Odysseus' making a semicircle with his plow around his infant son, Telemachus, who had been thrown in front of his plow by Palamedes in order to demonstrate Odysseus' sanity and therefore his suitability to serve in the Trojan wars. Odysseus had feigned insanity in an effort not to have to leave his wife and son, wishing to participate fully in his child's upbringing. When parents value their children and support with pride their lustful and aggressive strivings, Kohut holds there is no need for the child to repress its instinctual life so that neurotic personality organization results.

The second mythic theme is associated with a listening perspective first envisioned by Freud (1914) but more fully elaborated by Kohut (1971, 1977). This way of listening to another person is suggested by the way Narcissus discovered of confirming himself through studying his reflection. Three-year-olds are in constant search of consolidation of their nascent selves by seeking mirroring, twinning, and idealizing relations with others. This mirror function sought out in others is experienced as an aspect of themselves. Kohut (1971) has called such self-confirming love objects "selfobjects." When the relatedness patterns of a person retain excessively this (3-year-old level) compulsion to search endlessly for self-confirmation, affirmation, and inspiration from the other, that person is thought to display a narcissistic personality organization.

The third perspective for listening to human relatedness potentials is the one most elaborated by Gillespie's work. This perspective for listening to the merged dual-identity relationship of mother and child is metaphorically derived from the developmental period from 4 to 24 months, called by Margaret Mahler, the "symbiosis" (1968). Mahler borrowed this metaphor from biology not so much to characterize the sociological relation of mother and child, as to portray the relatedness patterns that the child internalizes. The learning patterns or internal structuring of the symbiotic period can be thought of as a series of "scenarios" in which two come to automatically cue and respond to one another, almost as though they were one. Distinctions between (1) generations, (2) genders, (3) good and bad, and (4) inside and outside remain tenuous so that ordinary self and other contrasts often remain blurred, confused, or kaleidoscopic. Failure to make these distinctions in various ways is illustrated in Gillespie's text as well as in the visual productions she presents.

The mythic theme of the symbiotic period is expressed by the dual (split) nature of the Roman god Janus, the god of portals and beginnings.

The portal to human life is thought to be the symbiotic exchange through which the affective relation to human intelligence prepares the way for the later emergence of human symbolism, language, and culture. Entering the north portal of the Forum, Janus is portrayed as a beardless (sexless) youth; but once inside the space created by human intelligence, he is portrayed as a virile, fully matured man.

The text and illustrations to be encountered by the reader of this book portray many of the literally infinite aspects of the symbiotic relatedness patterns experienced by mother and child. As illustrations, they are provocative and cause us to consider many possible kinds of mothering experience and some of their implications for how people create their later lives from these significant interactional beginnings. Dyadic relatedness patterns established in the symbiotic period inevitably structure later interpersonal experience. But "good-enough mothering" helps the child relinquish rigid adherence to the private mother-child culture of relatedness and to expand his or her relating patterns toward independent selfhood and triadic relating. However, if the dyadic modes are extensively retained, the person may be seen as displaying a borderline personality organization.

The fourth listening perspective for understanding self and other relatedness patterns is also elaborated here by Gillespie's work and the vivid illustrations she provides. The origins of psyche are traceable to the later months in utero and to the earliest months of extrauterine life. The sensory-motor and perceptual capacities of the infant are optimally engaged in organizing channels of relatedness to the maternal body and the maternal person and mind. Mammals share the search for the warmth and nurturance offered by mother's body. Various forms of social organization have evolved among mammals to permit and foster that relationship. So that while relationship intelligence is not peculiar to humans, certainly human intelligence and culture foster the infant in its complex task of accommodation and acculturation to its human environment.

Depth psychology has associated failures in the establishment of a psychologically sustaining mother-child relationship with various forms of psychosis. The listening perspective for tuning into the earliest aspects of organizing meaningful channels for interpersonal connectedness focuses on the kinds of representations of selfness and otherness that express the infant's search for relatedness. But the critical dimension of this listening perspective is the way in which disconnectedness or the failure to connect safely to mother is represented. That is, if symbiotic relatedness begins human life as we know it, then depth psychology searches for the kinds of early developmental experience that may have foreclosed for the individual the possibility of symbiotic connectedness.

Kirk's "Mother and Child With Teeth" in Gillespie's chapter on mother-and-child portrayals by artists is a vivid representation of the kinds of issues that might prevent the establishment of a comfortable and safe symbiotic relationship. The mythic theme that captures the spirit of the organizing period of human development is expressed in the myth of Proteus, the god of social instincts who was capable of assuming all forms and who knew all things past, present, and future. This sense of timelessness and the infinity of possible forms expresses the situation of the infant searching to organize meaningful paths to achieve a sense of social organization. Proteus taught Aristaeus how to honor the gods and then how to domesticate colonies of bees. A person not able to organize his or her instinctual nature into social patterns continues abortively to search for bonding, organizing connections throughout life. This inability to find a mother to organize with is portrayed in Gillespie's work.

The self and other relatedness paradigm now pursued by psychoanalysts and other persons interested in depth psychology no longer requires a medical orientation based on illness and cure, as the search for psychic representation takes center stage. No longer is an objective, scientific orientation required since a systematic study of subjectivity is what allows a person access to his or her inner governing representational patterns. The search for the historical truth of a person's childhood is now relinquished in favor of developing various relational and narrational contexts expressed in the elaboration of self and other representations. The mythical beasts encountered in psychopathology texts can now be set aside in favor of a personal search for patternings of one's representational world. The four watersheds of human relatedness reconceptualized as perspectives for listening to personally constructed representational worlds also permits a technical shift in psychoanalysis from the traditional frame technique to variable responsiveness techniques. That is, earlier developmental modes require empathic response that is appropriate to their preverbal nature.

Gillespie's work elaborates our understanding of contemporary depth psychology. Her contribution is a significant one in that it allows us to visualize complex self and other representations. The representations of the mother-child relationship that are provided here in words and picture, stimulate the reader's imagination to envision the many ways individual experience can be structured in personality.

For readers interested in psychotherapy and psychoanalysis this text opens a vista of possibilities for representations of transference and countertransference. For readers interested in diagnostics the text amply demonstrates the kind of interpretive possibilities inherent in mother-and-child drawings. For readers searching to experience the depth of the mother-and-child relationship or simply to enjoy delightful portrayals of the first love relationship, these pages will be rewarding.

REFERENCES

Freud, S. (1900). *The interpretation of dreams.* New York: Avon Books.

Freud, S. (1901). The psychopathology of everyday life. *The standard edition of the complete psychological works of Sigmund Freud, 6.* London: The Hogarth Press and the Institute of Psycho-Analysis.

Freud, S. (1905). Jokes and their relation to the unconscious. *Standard edition, 7*:3-124.

Freud, S. (1914). On narcissism. *Standard edition, 14*:69.

Freud, S. (1923). The ego and the id. *Standard edition, 19*:3-68.

Hartmann, H. (1939–1958). *Ego psychology and the problem of adaptation.* New York: International Universities Press.

Jacobson, E. (1964). *The self and the object world.* New York: International Universities Press.

Kohut, H. (1971). *The analysis of the self.* New York: International Universities Press.

Kohut, H. (1977). *The restoration of the self.* New York: International Universities Press.

Kohut, H. (1982). Introspection, empathy and the semi-circle of mental health. *International Journal of Psychoanalysis, 63*:395-407.

Mahler, M. (1968). *On human symbiosis and the vicissitudes of individuation,* Vol. I. *Infantile psychosis.* New York: International Universities Press.

Acknowledgments

The drawings in this book have been collected over a period of several years, and it is completely impossible for me even to begin to thank the many, many colleagues, as well as graduate students in psychology at California Graduate Institute, who have contributed drawings to my now substantial collection, only a few of which can be included herein. I still thoroughly enjoy receiving new ones, with the usual enthusiastic preface, "Wait till you see *this*!"

For those of us who love patient drawings, it has always been rather like that, and this new mode of drawing has provided some additional wonderful moments of insight and raised new questions to guide us in our work.

I must offer a special word of thanks here to Ida Stolk, whose delinquent population in a correctional facility has provided some particularly interesting material.

Words fail me as I try to think of an appropriate thank you to Larry Hedges, an extraordinary psychoanalyst, master teacher, and supervisor. He has been more than generous in his support for this project, and his perceptions always invite me further along the way in my own explorations. His foreword to this book enriches it immeasurably.

Jeff Levine's contribution to this book, though indirect, has been substantial. His careful and patient monitoring of my struggles with this material and his unfailing warmth and support have been even more important than his analytic insights.

I am particularly grateful to two internationally known artists who have generously permitted photos of their work to be included herein: Juan Ferrandiz, of Barcelona, Spain, and Paul Nzambala, originally of Uganda and now working in Los Angeles. Both of these men have shared not only wonderful materials but also their personal time for comment. I am not surprised by their generosity of spirit, however, since their mother-and-child art pieces suggest the inner strength and givingness in relationships that the thesis of this book would predict.

Special thanks are due to the University of Minnesota Press, which has granted me permission to reproduce the adapted version of the Minnesota Multiphasic Personality Inventory (MMPI) profile sheets found in Chapter 5, and to International Universities Press, which has granted me permission to reprint the fascinating drawings by Peter Heller from *A Child Analysis with Anna Freud* in Chapter 1.

Portions of the material in this book are reprinted from *Arts in Psychotherapy*, Vol. 16, Jacquelyn Gillespie, "Object relations as observed in mother-and-child drawings," pp. 163–70, (1989), with kind permission from Pergamon Press, Ltd., Headington Hill Hall, Oxford OX3 OBW, UK.

My family has offered major resources of time and assistance to this work. My son has sent me mother-and-child drawings from Thailand, and my daughter, with amazing patience, has responded to my frequent cries of distress when my level of competence with the word processor is not up to demand. (She now mothers me well.) My husband, Tom Gillespie, has provided the most important support of all—unfailing nurturing and caring over many years of "good mothering." I am immeasurably grateful to them all.

My most special thanks are saved for Natalie Gilman, extraordinary editor, who has managed to combine a generous and thoughtful awareness of concepts with an unfailing eye for detail. She has saved me from myself over and over again.

The Projective Use of Mother-and-Child Drawings

A MANUAL FOR CLINICIANS

CHAPTER 1

Theoretical Issues Affecting Mother-and-Child Drawings

The material presented here on mother-and-child drawings differs from the usual material on person and family drawings in that it is based on a particular theoretical notion—the notion that the projective aspect of the drawings can yield a special portrait of the self. Not the social self, or the one that the "I" can recognize as "I," but the self that is somehow developed in the earliest days and years of life through the link between child and mother. Object relations theory defines that earliest interaction as the source of the self-perceptions and style of relating to others that become part of the maturing and adult personality.*

A FEW NOTES ON OBJECT RELATIONS THEORY

The Mother and Child in Psychoanalytic Thought

The importance of mother in the psychological development of the child has always been a fundamental tenet of classical psychoanalysis and has been further developed through the work of Fairbairn (1954), Melanie

* For those who wish to avoid theoretical considerations, a brief summary of the guiding principles underlying the use of mother-and-child drawings as a projective technique appears at the beginning of Chapter 4.

Klein (1948/1975) and her followers, Winnicott (1965, 1971/1980) and the "Independent Group" in analysis, and the foundation work in ego psychology as developed by Anna Freud (1965, 1937/1966), Hartmann (1964), Jacobson (1964), and Spitz (1965).

The work of Mahler, Pine, and Bergman (1975) has served to give an impetus to the consideration of mother-and-child issues by others than those steeped in psychoanalytic traditions. For one thing, the work of Mahler and collaborators is based on practical, clinical observation of mothers and children behaving toward each other in ways that can be monitored and objectively assessed. Through their graphic descriptions of children clinging, pulling away, moving toward and/or against mother, leaving her to explore and then rushing back again—all in definable developmental sequences based on satisfyingly large samples—we are presented with a reality of a mother-child developmentally sequential relationship rather like that found in the Piagetian child development literature. The solid ground of observation lends credibility to and provides new interest in Mahler's psychoanalytic formulations concerning early child development.

The major theme of the Mahler and coauthors' (1975) work is the complementarity of symbiosis and individuation in the very early intrapsychic development of the child. They posit a universal initial "symbiotic" phase that is developmentally normal and that slowly gives way to a separation-individuation phase, which is then followed in the normal course of things by other steps toward an individual sense of self and object constancy. Developmental disruption, particularly in the separation-individuation phase, results in identity conflicts that may be reactivated through eliciting events at any stage of life. These conflicts may become the focus of many clinical hours of psychotherapy.

It is not the place of this material to go into the issues of object relations in any detail. There are prominent theorists and a wide variety of publications available for the interested reader. For those who are new to the concept, a useful introductory volume is Guntrip's *Psychoanalytic Theory, Therapy, and the Self* (1971). The suggested reading list at the end of this book may also prove helpful.

Contrasting Interpersonal Relationships Theory and Object Relations Theory

There are a number of basic issues that underlie the development of mother-and-child drawings that are object relations concerns; there are also certain common misconceptions about object relations that need to be addressed.

At first glance, the issues of the earliest mother-and-child relationships appear to belong to those of a broader constellation of interpersonal relationships, perhaps along the lines established by Harry Stack Sullivan (1953). At a social level, that is true. But for object relations theory, the issues are quite different. And here is the fundamental difference of critical importance to understanding and interpreting mother-and-child drawings from an object relations perspective:

The study of interpersonal relationships is an exercise in social and cognitive psychology, where real people engage in real encounters, real communications, real transactions. Those people are aware of what they are doing, for the most part, and if they are not, then they can be instructed and their ignorance alleviated. New information is accepted and integrated with old, and new behaviors result. Habit patterns may be very difficult to change, but the potential is there and dealt with through practice and new learning or with reward systems.

The study of object relations, in contrast, deals with internal images of external reality that are colored by experience. From this point of view, there are no "real" perceptions of others, since all perceptions are selective in nature and filtered through memories and anticipations. We therefore construct internal representations or "objects" that we relate to as if they accurately represent the persons, and our experience of them, in the external world.

The earliest relationship in life is the mother-and-child relationship. Because the human infant has experienced the nine months before birth in the most intimate contact with mother, and since that contact remains the primary one in the child's introduction to the world, a concept of "mother" gradually develops that represents the first understanding of the world. At that time the world remains simply an extension of the self, and mother is seen as the source of sustenance and soothing. But mother also is not always there, and pain and other unpleasant events occur, and the baby must make some adaptation to that fact. Experiencing mother as both good and bad develops a prototype for later experiences of others and, even more important, for the perception of the self.

The power of that earliest relationship, says object relations theory, can hardly be overestimated. The sense of self derived from that relationship forms the basis for all subsequent relationships and also forms the expectations of the world. In this experience the child develops the first fantasies of the self and the "other," the object that is the internal subjective representation of mother (later, the "others" out there), who can never be experienced directly. The initial internal object formations are preverbal and largely unconscious and continue to influence later conscious thought processes.

Another related concept is that of self-as-object, a useful way of conceptualizing the ability to identify with the mother and thereby gain control of the child-self (see Bollas, 1987).

The Object Relations Outlook in Psychotherapy

According to Winnicott (1971/1980), "psychotherapy takes place in the overlap of two areas of playing, that of the patient and that of the therapist ... two people playing together" (p. 44). Winnicott sees play as the universal activity that opens up creativity and, in the therapy situation, offers the opportunity for communication. In many respects it replicates the early relationship with the mother, in which the mother attends carefully to the exploratory activities of the child and accepts the child's self-expression with pleasure.

Art therapy partakes to an unusually great extent of the kinds of affective interactions that were part of that early mother-and-child experience. The effective art therapist is comfortable in that shared play space, not the physical space in which the art activities occur, but in a shared subjective world space that in later life retains the mutuality of the early mother and child relationship.

Winnicott (1971/1980) calls this space the "transitional space," which provides safety and the opportunity for self-expression. It is possible for the therapist to show the same kind of acceptance of patient output that mother gave—or should have given—to the young child's creativity.

Assessment settings do not provide the time or opportunity for the mutual exploration that is so powerful an aspect of ongoing therapy, but the impact of a drawing is often strong enough to make it seem that a drawing is indeed worth a thousand words.

The elusive inner self lies somewhere at the heart of psychological assessments. It is also the search for that self that is central to the work of psychotherapy.

"Mommy and I Are One": A Validation Study

In recent years there have been a number of attempts to validate psychoanalytic concepts through the techniques of experimental psychology. Perhaps the most important of those for the issues raised here are the detailed studies of Silverman, Lachmann, and Milich (1982), summarized with critiques by them in 1984 for an analytic audience, and summarized more generally in Silverman and Weinberger (1985). Through the medium of tachistoscopic presentation of a subliminal stimulus of the phrase "Mommy and I Are One," along with a pictorial image of two human figures joined at the shoulders, the researchers were able to evoke changes in behavior and test response in schizophrenic and other patient groups.

Designed specifically to test the notions of merger and fusion between mother and child inherent in the concept of symbiosis through the use of a "oneness" stimulus, the results of the primary study with schizophrenics found that "more differentiated" patients showed improvement, whereas "less differentiated" patients showed no reduction in pathology. The more differentiated patients were presumably able to maintain separateness while profiting from the oneness experience; on the other hand, the less differentiated patients were unable to do so because of what seemed to be a threat to the sense of self. Differentiation, in this study, was described as "level of differentiation from mother" and defined through patient rating scales of self and mother and the degree to which the ratings coincided (Silverman, Lachmann, & Milich, 1984).

This ingenious study of schizophrenics and subsequent work with a number of other patient and nonpatient groups provided evidence that issues of symbiosis can be explored usefully in an experimental fashion. The portion of the Silverman material described here, however, has identified the differentiation of self from mother as a relevant variable in the examination of issues of symbiosis and suggests its validity as a clinical concern. It is the Silverman thesis that "oneness gratifications enhance adaptation only if a sense of self is preserved" (Silverman & Weinberger, 1985, p. 1300).

If Silverman and his colleagues have been able to demonstrate issues of symbiosis and differentiation through the use of rating scales and responses to subliminal stimulation, then is it not possible that such concerns may also be clinically accessible through the use of projective mother-and-child drawings?

THE DEVELOPMENT OF PROJECTIVE DRAWING TECHNIQUES

Origins of Projective Drawings

Although the work of artists and patient art work had for some time been of interest to psychologists, the systematic use of patient drawings as expressions of self-concept, affective states, and various kinds of pathology originated with the work of Machover (1949), who used draw-a-person figures to evoke evidence of "the impulses, anxieties, conflicts, and compensations characteristic of that individual" (p. 35).

In the course of evaluating children with the Goodenough (1926) Draw-a-Man test to determine IQ, she found that the drawings yielded so much clinical data that she soon included person drawings regularly in child assessment batteries and then extended them to adult assessments as well. The drawings were evaluated in conjunction with clinical data and associations given by the subjects, and principles were derived governing interpretation. Those principles were set forth in some detail in Machover's monograph and have set the basic standard for the continuing clinical use of drawings in assessment and psychotherapy.

Variations in Projective Drawing Techniques

There have, of course, been a number of variations over the years on the technique established by Machover. The House-Tree-Person technique, developed by Buck and first published in 1948, appeared at about the same time as Machover's work.

Family drawings have also been used with children for many years (Reznikoff & Reznikoff, 1956; Oster & Gould, 1987). A subsequent and very popular variation, known as the Kinetic Family Drawing (Burns & Kaufman, 1970, 1972; Burns, 1982) specifically focuses on "your family" and the interaction among family members.

There have been other modifications of the basic Draw-a-Person technique, but none has been of particular significance in terms of the type of response required. However, a most creative and different approach to a projective person drawing was developed by Malchiodi (1990) in the course of her work with abused children. Malchiodi has children draw a "full-size person on a large piece of white butcher paper cut to the approximate size of the child" (p. 118). This Life-Size-Body Drawing (LSBD) is not a body tracing, but an actual drawing task that parallels the usual draw-a-person activity. Says Malchiodi,

> This may contribute to the level of energy and investment required to engage in and complete such an activity. Preliminary observations indicate that children related more directly to the life-size image, and showed increased verbalization, and a higher interest level in participating in the task. Perhaps the life-size image, because it approximates the child's size and therefore is more like the child, is more projective. (p.117)

This technique offers considerable promise. However, Malchiodi warns that "confrontational aspects of the large self-image may be overwhelming" (p. 120) in some cases and suggests caution in its use and careful provision for support and follow-up.

None of these techniques appear to have addressed the issues of theory in any depth. In fact, although Machover (1949) comments that there is "an intimate tie-up between the figure drawn and the personality of the individual who is doing the drawing" (p. 4), she is vague on the nature of that tie-up. She goes ahead to say that "some process of selection involving identification through projection and introjection enters at some point" (p. 5). Her speculations largely involve the use of a person drawing as a physical activity, drawing on an inner body image, that provides a "natural vehicle" for the expression of a person's body needs and conflicts. However, she points out that the technique was developed in clinics and hospitals as "a clinical tool for personality analysis, rather than around any theoretical hypotheses" (p. 20).

Validation of Projective Drawing Techniques

In Harris's (1963) evaluation of various materials on children's drawings, he comments on the projective use of drawings: "In terms of theory, this field of research has been quite diffuse. Rather than scientifically analytical, its proponents have tended toward intuitive impressionism" (p. 11).

The terms "projection" and "introjection," as well as Machover's frequent use of the term "unconscious," suggest some basic reliance on psychoanalytic thought. In fact, a recent and comprehensive summary of a host of drawing techniques by Oster and Gould (1987) finds the derivations of the procedure in the work of Freud, Kris, and Jung in their concerns with the creative mind and unconscious processes and goes ahead to describe the development of art therapy as, originally, an adjunct to psychoanalysis.

In spite of this bow to psychoanalytic thought, in the interpretation of the material there is nowhere any systematic application of analytic principles. Pictorial representations are often taken at face value, but then they are also often depicted as representing defenses. The interpretation may flow from one to another without acknowledging that important transition. Even more important, perhaps, is the lack of systematic reference to transference, countertransference, and resistance issues in the psychological literature related to drawings. Recently, the art therapy literature, with its roots more specifically in psychoanalytic theory, has begun to address these issues (e.g., Schaverien, 1992; Simon, 1992).

As Harris points out, clinicians appear to work intuitively, referring to other information available about the individual to support or contradict the data from the drawing. Clinically, this is a useful approach and certainly utilizes the important principle that conclusions should never be made from drawings alone (or any other projective material, for that matter).

However, the multiple possible interpretations that can be made from just about any art material call into serious question the clinical use of "cookbook" or "dictionary" sorts of interpretations of characteristics of drawings that can be found in some publications (e.g., Gilbert, 1978; Hammer, 1964; Jolles, 1964; Wenck, 1977). However, the early House-Tree-Person research done by Hammer was extremely important in that it probably made the first serious attempt to objectify and quantify the many possible interpretations of drawing characteristics on the basis of frequency of certain characteristics in specific populations, such as large teeth or sharply pointed fingers in aggressive prisoners, and various varieties of sexual symbolism in the drawings of eugenically sterilized subjects. Jolles carefully developed a comprehensive catalog of drawing characteristics in an attempt to systematize the vast amount of interpretive data that was accumulating at the time.

Both researchers underlined the problems associated with indiscriminate use of their materials. Koppitz (1968), who catalogued the characteristics of children's human figure drawings, also urged caution in their use. However, the potential for misuse by beginning or poorly trained clinicians remains high.

Anastasi (1982), in the fifth edition of her authoritative work on psychological testing, continues to reiterate her earlier comments on the lack of consistent validation support for the use of the Draw-a-Person Test and suggests that it should be considered "part of a clinical interview, in which the drawings are interpreted in the context of other information about the individual" (p. 580).

Over the years, since the early work by Machover and Buck, there have been many attempts to validate the clinical use of drawings and many studies attempting to find specific drawing characteristics in delimited populations (e.g., Bieliauskas, 1980; Di Leo, 1973; Harrower, Thomas, & Altman, 1975; Kay, 1978; Kellogg, 1979; Miljkovitch & Irvine, 1982; Rubin, Ragins, Schachter, & Wimberly, 1979; Schildkrout, Shenker, & Sonnenblick, 1972; Wysocki & Wysocki, 1977). The results continue to be equivocal.

Although these caveats suggest careful and prudent interpretation of all projective drawing materials, they should not discourage use of the large body of what might be called the basic interpretations in common use in the evaluation of projective drawings. This material (e.g., shading as representing anxiety, buttons down the front as dependency, sharply pointed fingernails as aggression) is observed so frequently by therapists as to have achieved over the years a sort of basic communicative language about drawing interpretation. On the other hand, idiosyncratic interpretations such as rear emphasis reflecting homosexuality in males (buttocks emphasis, auto tail lights, back porch lights) are much more suspect and clearly dangerous if accepted uncritically.

As the various projective drawing techniques have developed over the last 30 years, it is clear that pragmatic validation, rather than research confirmation, of the interpretations has been the source of their popularity and utility in clinical experience. Theory has been sparse and of little importance.

It seems that the early attempts to provide research confirmation for all sorts of characteristics of person drawings met with so little success that the attempts to consider these techniques as "tests" within the usual limits of the term have largely been discontinued. Anastasi's (1982) advice to use the materials as a part of a clinical interview seems particularly apt in the use of mother-and-child drawings. The communication potential of the device is high, but each drawing is highly individual and a means of communication within the assessment or therapy relationship.

CONSCIOUS AND UNCONSCIOUS ASPECTS OF DRAWINGS

Interpersonal relationships are the subject matter of cognitive psychologies, behavior modification, and family system theories. These cognitive interpretations are the ones most prominently found in books on interpretations of drawings. However, these notions are often mixed indiscriminately with psychoanalytic formulations resting on such basic analytic concepts as the unconscious.

For example, here are some comments by Oster and Gould (1987) in a section talking about drawings as projective techniques:

> For instance, children who view themselves as having greater significance in the family when compared to siblings will likely place themselves in greater proximity to the parents. In marked contrast, children feeling isolated or different from their siblings might draw themselves off to one side or not participating in a family activity. (p. 18)

From an object relations point of view, a number of unconscious processes may be involved in family drawings that also need to be considered as possible interpretations. For example, the child who draws herself standing next to mother may be drawing a wish fulfillment and exiling mother's real favorite to a place outside the family circle. It is not unusual to observe abused children drawing families with nice, attentive parents in scenes that are clearly, from other information, not realistic.

In other words, some of the drawings reflect an individual's sense of real social relationships, and others may include unconscious intrapsychic relations and feelings. A child might look at a drawing in which he has drawn a big brother, with whom he seems in perpetual conflict, as a tiny figure about to be eaten by the family dog—and talk about it in completely innocuous terms. "Oh, they always play like that." On further questioning, he might recount, with some relish, an event in which the dog had indeed attacked the brother and caused him to have 16 stitches in his arm. To go even further, he might also report feeling that he, himself, is the tiny one and helpless before his brother's power and aggression.

Because it is usually possible to validate some of the issues presented in drawings from other sources, professionals often feel safe in drawing conclusions—and they may be incorrect. Children involved in custody battles, for example, often worry about alienating parents and try to draw accordingly—sometimes deliberately and sometimes unconsciously. Validating information obtained from parents in those situations is highly suspect, since the parents are in no position to be objective about the child's relationship with the other parent. Yet that situation is one in which children's drawings are often used to help make important custody decisions.

It is also important to be careful about the instructions in family drawings. The instruction to "draw a family" is very much like that to "draw a person." It does not specify what family or what person and can therefore elicit an idealized family or various wish fulfillments. The younger the child, the more concrete the thinking, and very young children almost always draw themselves or their own families, as they usually announce. The "draw-a-person" or "draw-a-family" instructions need to be used deliberately, with careful observation and a wary eye for hidden projections.

Contemporary blended families, with all sorts of relationships as part of present and past families, are wonderful subjects for family drawings. In order to get a real sense of object relations, it is important to give the instructions "draw a family" in just those words. Which family the child decides to draw is instructive. Sometimes a child will mix in a former half-brother in what appears to be a current family constellation. It is important not to tell the child that she has made a mistake—she really has not made a mistake and is simply letting you know that the half-brother still feels like a member of the family to her.

Instructions to "draw *your* family" evoke a more social, cognitive appraisal of the family and will probably be more detailed and realistic. It will be, of course, less projective in nature, since projection is a term that means the attribution of unconscious inner feelings to others.

In fact, Burns (1982) illustrates the point quite well in his description of the development of the Kinetic-Family-Drawing technique:

> I had the patient draw-a-person (D-A-P), an old psychological test by Goodenough ... and the "person" reflected a self-image. If that didn't work, ... I would give a House-Tree-Person test and get three more self-portraits....
>
> A friendly but skeptical medical resident suggested that if I wanted a self-portrait, why not be direct and ask for one? So the Kinetic-Family-Drawing technique began in which a self-portrait was drawn in a kinetic family matrix.
>
> After gathering some K-F-Ds and comparing them to the D-A-Ps it was evident the resident was correct; *the person obtained in the D-A-P was usually unlike the "self" obtained in the K-F-D* [italics added]. (p. 19)

However, those differences do not show that the D-A-P is less useful than the K-F-D. They simply measure different things. The D-A-P is more open to unconscious influences, and the K-F-D is more involved with the conscious attempt to present an external reality. The differences noted by Burns in a series of drawing comparisons are quite interesting.

Returning, now, to the Oster and Gould (1987) material:

> When a request is made to draw a tree, an assumption is made that the tree reflects deeper and possibly more *unconscious* feelings [italics added] about the self. It seems easier in this case to ascribe a greater amount of less desirable personal traits to an inanimate object since it appears more removed from a self-description. (p. 18)

It is easier to see the tree as a receptacle for projections than human figure drawings, as the author points out. However, the cognitive objective framework for interpretation has now been replaced by a subjective analytic one. The next comment, however, refers to human figure drawings: "The drawing of a person, of course, reflects a more direct expression of real life feelings" (p. 18). Perhaps, but the drawing of the person may also contain considerable unconscious projection. All drawings, of course, depict a combination of perceptions and projections. In the art of interpretation, however, it is important to differentiate the two as much as possible.

PROJECTION IN PATIENT DRAWINGS

Patient drawings, like those of acknowledged skilled artists, are creative works of nonverbal imagination. They are completely subjective, and therein lies their projective significance. However, like the work of artists, they may also be seen to project wishes and fears or to deny unpleasant realities. It is not unusual, for example, for children who are known to be in a family in severe poverty to draw a person in elaborate clothes and jewels. It would be absurd for examiners to consider such pictures as evidence that the family is really quite affluent.

Splitting may be seen better in mother-and-child drawings. That is, a mother who is in treatment to conquer habits of verbal abuse frequently directed toward her children may draw a sweetly smiling child with an angry, screaming mother or a furious child with a blandly serene mother. In such a situation the discrepancy between the figures suggests the need to explore issues of splitting and projective identification as well as the actual home circumstances that may lead to verbal abuse. Here the differentiation may be considered to be negative rather than positive, in that it is not appropriate to have one party to a relationship smiling in the face of so much anger. In such a clinical situation it would be particularly helpful to have drawings from the child as well as the mother to compare and contrast their presentations of self and other.

TRANSFERENCE, COUNTERTRANSFERENCE, AND RESISTANCE IN DRAWINGS AND THEIR INTERPRETATION

Projective drawings are obtained in an encounter between two individuals who must form some sort of relationship with each other, however brief.

There are two primary situations in which drawings are used by clinicians: (1) as a projective assessment technique, which is usually done by someone other than an ongoing therapist and as a one-time activity, and (2) in art therapy, in which a relationship develops that is of the same kind as one engendered in any other form of ongoing therapy. Obviously, in assessment work the clinician does not encounter the forms of transference that build over a period of time in a therapeutic relationship.

Transference issues are considered at the heart of psychotherapy from an object relations perspective. It is in the relationship with the therapist that the important early relationships have a chance to be experienced once again in a reparative form.

An unusual close glimpse of that relationship as it developed between a child and a famous therapist gives us the opportunity to understand something of that experience. Peter Heller, now a professor of German and European literature at the State University of New York at Buffalo, was a 9-year-old boy in Vienna when he was analyzed by Anna Freud early in her career. His recent account of that part of his life (Heller, 1990) is the fascinating encounter between a child and his therapist as they try to work through issues of parental separation and a mother who had left home.

The book includes drawings done by young Peter during the course of therapy, and there are many drawings there that touch on current object relations issues, although they were not so understood at the time. In fact, the two of them shown here (Figures 1.1 and 1.2) are mother-and-child drawings.

Heller's (1990) own annotations about Figure 1.1 say: "Fiercely marching girl or woman ... below: a small, intimidated creature" (p. 66). Although she may be "fiercely marching," it looks as though her heels are dug in and she is resisting forward movement, but there is no doubt about the "small, intimidated creature" below. The faint child-figure, who looks out with one large eye and another rudimentary one, appears caught up and engulfed by the huge mother-figure as she marches along. Perhaps her concomitant resistance reflects some of the ambivalence that must surround the feelings of a child caught up in family struggles. But more important, it would seem that the powerful woman partakes of some of the attributes of Anna Freud, who may indeed be leading the forward movement in the boy's development against considerable resistance, both conscious and unconscious. This portrayal seems to illustrate the transference, in which the incorporation of the therapist takes place as an aspect of the internal representation of the mother.

In Figure 1.2, the mother-figure is much less well defined and is trailed by a small figure floating along behind. Heller (1990) labels it "woman in twilight" [translated from the German for the English edition]. He parenthetically adds "(mother?)," and goes on to say she is being "persecuted by a little child-creature" (p. 46).

Figure 1.1. Mother and Child, Heller–a (Reprinted with permission from *A Child in Analysis with Anna Freud* [S. Burckhardt & M. Weigand, Trans. (revised by the author)], by P. Heller. By permission of International Universities Press, Inc. Copyright © 1990 by International Universities Press, Inc.).

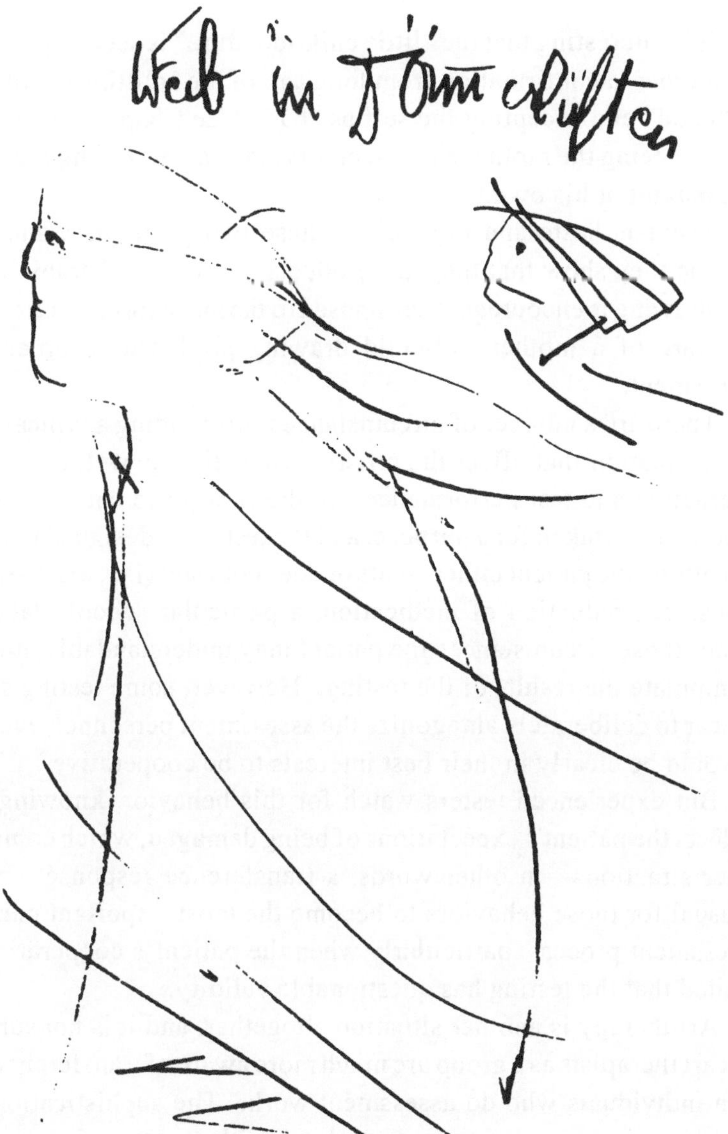

Figure 1.2. Mother and Child, Heller–b (Reprinted with permission from *A Child in Analysis with Anna Freud* [S. Burckhardt & M. Weigand, Trans. (revised by the author)], by P. Heller. By permission of International Universities Press, Inc. Copyright © 1990 by International Universities Press, Inc.).

It is interesting that the "little child-creature" is seen as persecuting the mother, a confirmation from long ago of the splitting off of mother as "good" and accepting the self as "bad" (see Chapter 5). The child avoids seeing the mother as persecutory, instead accepting the badness and making it his own.

There is haste and urgency in these two portrayals, and in that fashion they show that they are products of ongoing therapy in which free drawing is encouraged, as opposed to the more formal and complete structure of a mother-and-child drawing produced to order during assessment.

There are a number of circumstances surrounding a typical assessment situation that affect the artistic production as well as the verbal interaction and test performance. In the first place, an assessment is usually undertaken for a purpose, and the testing is designed to produce something the patient either wants or does not want (i.e., discharge from a hospital, reduction of medication, a particular school placement). Under those circumstances the patient may understandably attempt to manipulate the results of the testing. However, some testing subjects appear to deliberately antagonize the assessment personnel, even when it would be clearly in their best interests to be cooperative.

But experienced testers watch for this behavior, knowing that it reflects the patient's expectations of being damaged, which comes from other situations—in other words, a transference response. It is not unusual for those behaviors to become the most important part of the assessment process, particularly when the patient's cooperation is so limited that the testing has questionable validity.

Art therapy is another situation altogether, and it is not surprising that art therapists as a group are much more aware of transference issues than individuals who do assessment work. The sophistication of art therapists in recognizing and working with the transference varies tremendously, however. The concept of transference, although treated extensively only in the psychoanalytic literature, has been readily accepted from many clinical perspectives, since it is clear that reactions to the therapist are often "out of the blue" and not necessarily related directly to the actual behavior of the therapist.

Transference Issues

Transference, briefly stated, is the body of ideas and prejudices with accompanying affects that an individual brings into a new relationship from previous relationships. These largely unconscious influences tend to color and obscure the development of the new situation. This sort of thing affects all relationships inescapably. Every new relationship must somehow deal with the past.

However, transference assumes a special meaning in the therapeutic setting. Here, with an accepting therapist, a person is able to express feelings not acceptable in a standard social situation. All therapists have been subjected to blasts of rage, tears, and scenes from people who are either out of control or close to it. They are told that they are unfeeling, heartless beasts; they are cruel, uncaring, dominating, and controlling. And on and on. Therapists routinely accept and try to understand these feelings that derive from previous relationships and make that understanding a major part of the therapeutic work.

The lack of validity of the feelings expressed in this kind of negative transference is easier for the therapist to understand and acknowledge than the unrealistic quality of the feelings that may accompany a positive transference. After all, the therapist needs the personal reassurance that all those terrible accusations have no basis in reality; once that is understood, the therapeutic search for the origins of those hostile feelings can begin.

On the other hand, an idealizing transference feels good; it helps make up for having to endure all the negatives. When a patient tells the therapist "You're wonderful!" the therapist is not so inclined to question the basis for the adoration. Once in a while the positive transference turns into a full-blown love obsession. If not recognized and responded to effectively early enough, it can become the basis for some of the lawsuits that plague the mental health profession. Unrequited love evokes fury and the desire for revenge, wherever it is found.

Therapists count on a certain amount of positive transference to make their work possible; a person believed unable to form a transference relationship has often been considered an unsuitable candidate for intensive psychotherapy. Even in assessment work, an occasional individual seems to resist the tasks either actively or in some sort of passive fashion so intensely that the examiner strongly feels that the assessment is lacking in validity. (See the *Resistance* section in this chapter.) Sometimes the examiner has nothing specific to go on in defending that notion; however, those feelings should receive careful attention. The examiner's sense of passive resistance on the part of the examinee, particularly when it is hard to describe or defend, is often a mark of transference and an indication of the person's defensive style, which may be extremely subtle. "I'll give you nothing" is a clear message that has undoubtedly been given elsewhere before, and, if so, also received from someone significant in earlier life. Perhaps in equally subtle ways.

In art therapy some of the most typical defenses simply do not work. People who have managed to erect elaborate verbal defenses are often at a loss when confronted with pencils, paper, paint, or clay. Art therapists find a certain kind of vulnerability in their patients, then, that allows them to bypass a certain kind of superficiality that goes along with new verbal relationships. Children, of course, usually love art experiences of all kinds. Adults have become wary about self-exposure and are accustomed to retreating behind words. The art therapist knows that the first steps toward a working transference have been made when a patient produces some sort of creative effort and receives the therapist's acceptance. Sometimes fear of self-revelation is hidden behind aggressive behavior with art materials: "If I tear up the paper, break the crayons, and throw the clay on the floor, no one will laugh at me for what I would have produced." This outlook and defensive style is extremely common in acting-out children. They elicit anger for what they do to avoid the anger they expect for who they are.

One of the reasons for the growth of art therapy as a profession has been the recognition in the mental health community of the limits of the "talk therapies." Hammer (1986), who has remained for many years one of the primary figures in the projective drawings literature, states:

> Life was before language. The pictorial, drawing on a process that preceded language, retains more of the juices of feelings. And so children and adolescents relate more to, put more of themselves into, graphic than verbal projective techniques. (p. 240)

Artistic expression of all sorts avoids the necessity of finding the right words to express the pain that is, in itself, nonverbal. Psychological examiners have only a brief time in which to establish an interaction that yields diagnostic information. On the other hand, art therapists watch the growth of the artistic expression over a series of sessions, during which the transference relationship also emerges.

A particularly interesting point of view on transference and art has been presented by Schaverien (1992), who sees a piece of patient art itself as a transference object wherein the patient projects unconscious concerns and communications to the therapist. The therapist, in turn, responds. The art produced in what Schaverien terms "analytical art psychotherapy," takes place during an art therapy session that evokes both transference and countertransference interactions. The patient not only produces the picture but also has the opportunity to become the viewer, to step back, observe, and reflect on its meaning with the help of the therapist. Says Schaverien (1992),

> The picture offers an alternative external presence, it is an object which exists outside of the artist, and yet a part of her or him temporarily inhabits it....When the picture is finished ... the viewer comes to the fore and the artist watches, as if from a distance, while the viewer responds to the picture. (p. 19)

Schaverien likens this process to a kind of self-analysis that becomes part of the therapeutic process and occurs within the confines of the patient/therapist interaction. According to Schaverien,

> The unconscious of the client and that of the therapist may meet and mingle within the framed area of the picture. The effects of such a meeting reverberate within the whole wider meeting of the therapeutic context. Thus, the combination of client—picture—therapist may be a highly charged triangular encounter. (p. 119)

In many situations the work on these "highly charged" feelings may be subordinated to the demands of the treatment circumstances. Most therapists are working with individuals whose goals (or, at least, the goals of the caretakers) are for increased control and the skills to operate better in the real day-to-day world. To whatever extent the role of the therapist is that of parent to patient-child, the therapist-parent approves and rewards the occurrence of more coherent, more controlled, "better" drawings showing more positive feelings and less anger. Or perhaps the therapist rewards more self-expression on the part of the severely inhibited patient. In any case, if the positive transference is strong, the patient will work to produce what the therapist wants, just as the small child tries to please mommy. Therefore, one facet of the transference is to facilitate the emergence of behavior that the treating personnel desire.

Although behavioral change may be useful, it should be clearly understood that there may be less fundamental change in inner states to parallel the reinforced behavior than might be presumed. The art therapies, where there is a "product" to receive approval or disapproval, are quite susceptible to the problems associated with reinforcement, such as the transferability of response to other settings.

Countertransference Issues

The ability of the therapist to manipulate the response of the patient brings us to the issue of countertransference, which, like death, taxes, and transference, is always with us.

Like transference, in which the patient brings into the therapy situation a relationship history that is enacted once again in various ways during treatment, countertransference also brings historical material into the therapeutic relationship. This time the material belongs to the therapist.

Issues of countertransference are perhaps not so often recognized outside the parameters of psychoanalysis and psychoanalytic psychotherapy. "I can't stand that kid! I suppose he's not half as bad as some, but he's just the kind that really turns me off!" The dislike of the child in this case may contain elements of the therapist's countertransference, which, like transference, owes its existence to previous relationships and experiences.

However, countertransference may have serious consequences. After all, it is the therapist who holds the power in the relationship, and the patient is seldom in a position to challenge the attitudes of treating personnel. If possible, it is good professional practice for the therapist to refer patients toward whom feelings are unaccountably and uncommonly uncharitable. Therapists cannot work effectively with people who seem to evoke some sort of basic antipathy. The same is true for patients who evoke strong sexual responses or call forth way too much protectiveness, or evoke other evidence that full attention is not being given to their needs because therapist needs are getting in the way.

On the other hand, in the course of intense work with people, various feelings emerge on the part of the treating therapist that are actually engendered by the therapeutic interaction. They may at times stimulate the therapist's personal issues. Presumably, in the course of good training, the therapist has received enough psychotherapy to identify the primary sources of personal material that is likely to intrude on professional practice.

Traditionally, the existence of countertransference issues has been considered an annoyance or an impediment to the success of the therapy, to be banished if possible. Failing that, minimizing personal discomfort of the therapist has been the rule.

Kernberg (1975) discusses the concept of "totalistic" countertransference, defined as the total of "the analyst's conscious and unconscious reactions to the patient in the treatment situation" (p. 49). More recently a new perspective on the role of the countertransference in therapy has emerged. The work of Hedges (1983, 1992) offers the notion that the countertransference response of the therapist to the interaction with the patient can be highly instructive and facilitating to the therapy. He points out that the interactions in which the therapist is most uncomfortable evoke a struggle that can illustrate the kinds of painful interaction that are at the heart of the patient's relationship style and at the heart of the patient's distress. He has therefore moved the issue of the countertransference from a disruptive influence into a contributing factor in the therapeutic work.

This outlook offers a different approach to understanding transference and countertransference issues, noting the necessity of dealing with both as major areas of endeavor in therapy. These considerations offer a particular emphasis in working with drawings: whether in assessment or in ongoing art therapy, therapists have feelings about the art work that people produce that color the response to the people themselves.

Those feelings may skew interpretations in assessment work, sometimes with profound consequences. Those same feelings, in an ongoing art therapy situation, may either facilitate or inhibit the progress of the therapy. From the Hedges perspective, the therapist must attend closely to the countertransference feelings that are aroused in the interaction with the patient and in response to the art productions themselves.

It is there that the recent work of Schaverien (1992), discussed earlier in this chapter, is relevant. Her analytic art psychotherapy introduces not only the transference but also the countertransference as working tools within the art therapy situation. Important information about the patient's style of relating, replication of earlier forms of relatedness, and the ways in which the patient's defenses operate are often on display in many subtle ways that may be accessible only through the therapist's experience.

The circumstances of art therapy, unfortunately, may also lead to countertransference responses associated with other professional issues completely unrelated to the person in treatment. The therapist may have a personal agenda requiring apparent "improvement" in drawing proficiency and style. If the therapist is on the staff of an agency or hospital, it may seem important to present at case conferences patient work that will win the plaudits of the rest of the professional staff. If the therapist's position rests on certain types of artistic production from patients, then the work of therapy is certain to be seriously compromised.

Resistance Issues

The concept of resistance in therapy has traditionally been used to describe the ways in which individuals block recall of words, forget events, and otherwise distort memories associated with areas of conflict in the personality. However, this idea of resistance is based on the traditional psychoanalytic notions of unconscious conflicts related to sexual and aggressive drives and repressed impulses.

To include object relations concepts and developmental approaches within the framework of resistance expands the concept in several directions: (1) It reduces the emphasis on classic formulations of repression of unacceptable sexual or aggressive impulses; (2) it includes issues related to defense of identity and fears of relating to the therapist because of anticipated damage associated with early relationships; and (3) it permits focus on early developmental failures that become apparent in the style and extent of observed resistances. Blanck and Blanck (1974) discuss the "unmotivated patient" as exemplifying these issues.

In assessment work the apparently unmotivated individual presents as uninvolved, provides minimal responses, and goes through the required motions without expressing overt resistance, although the resistance can usually be inferred from that very lack of energy and involvement in the process. These are typically patients who provide stick drawings in Draw-a-Person or other person-drawing activities. Drawings with minimum detail also frequently fall in that category and must be distinguished from drawings with lack of detail associated with cognitive limitations.

Sometimes, in order to avoid stick-figure presentations of people, some examiners give instructions to draw "a whole person, and not a stick figure." However, in order to identify the expressive style of resistance, it is usually much more useful to use the open-ended approach. Just "Draw a person" or "Draw a mother and child" is enough. Then, if the patient produces stick figures, or just heads, it is always possible to request an additional drawing. The comparison is sometimes instructive.

In art therapy these individuals are initially reluctant to participate and, for some time, prefer to be given precise instructions or to copy the work of others in order to reduce the risk of self-exposure. It is important to note that the ways in which the initial reluctance is overcome and the growth of trust occurs uncover something about the patient's defensive style, as well as the therapist's work style. This activity becomes an important part of the therapy, rather than simply preparation for what has been traditionally considered the "real" work of the therapy. In this respect it parallels the more recent orientations to transference and countertransference, in which the therapist's self becomes increasingly important in the therapeutic process.

OBJECT RELATIONS ISSUES IN MOTHER-AND-CHILD DRAWINGS

Mother-and-child drawings were devised with direct consideration of object relations issues. The difficulty in sorting out projections from social perceptions is a specific problem for the art therapist or examiner who works with projective drawings. Mother-and-child drawings are designed not to avoid but to foster projections and identify perceptions of self and other that carry an unusually strong component of unconscious material.

In art therapy and in projective assessment through drawings, it becomes possible to take advantage of "our capacity to create visible symbols of things we comprehend unconsciously" (Simon, 1988, p. 51). The instructions to "draw a mother and child" are open-ended and allow portrayal of any form of representation that might be selected. Animal representations are found occasionally, and they offer fine opportunities for projection of all sorts of affective content.

There is sometimes a primary identification with either the mother- or the child-figure, which is thought to be identifiable in the use of stronger lines and more detail in one of the drawings. Children, logically enough, usually identify with the child-figure, and adult women with the mother-figure, whether or not they actually have children of their own. However, these conscious identifications are complicated by unconscious processes that appear to tap other levels of meaning. From an object relations perspective, each individual can at times identify with either of the figures, since either figure may become the subject or object, depending on internal or external circumstances.

Almost everyone draws the mother first—perhaps because the instructions put her first ("draw a mother and child"). A child drawn first is rare enough to suggest exploration.

Teenage girls typically start to identify with the mother-figure, whether consciously or not. Instead of an important well-detailed child-figure and a desexualized mother, all of a sudden the mother-figure starts to look like a teenager, and the child-figure is often a small baby in arms. In fact, that shift is of critical importance in identifying the psychological maturity level of the female teenager.

As might be expected, the drawing task is more difficult for teenage boys, who now want to disown identification with a child-figure but certainly don't want the alternative identification with the mother. This is the age when boys may solve the problem by using animal or other nonhuman figures. As the boy matures into the young man, he now, like the girl, will see the mother as a young woman (he is developing mature object relations) and the child as a baby in arms. Many men continue to have trouble with the mother-and-child portrayal, no doubt indicating some difficulty in internalizing women as positive objects. The problem is a common one.

Although the drawings can portray very vivid relationship patterns that reflect the "real" relationships between two individuals, it is useful to assume that both figures carry the projections of internalized self and other. For example, an individual (either adult or child) may draw a large fierce mother-figure and a very tiny smiling child. The inappropriateness of such a presentation suggests the probability that there is considerable internal conflict surrounding relationships involving nurturing and/or power, with denial as a probable defense.

The projection may be a transference issue related to the circumstances of the drawing. However, the individual's style of relating to others should be considered. Is this someone who smiles while under threat, or someone who appeases a powerful other? On the other hand, it is also important to look for the ways in which that anger is manifested. If a child draws hostile mother/passive child, the examiner cannot simply assume that the actual mother is the one who expresses the hostility and that the child is meek and submissive, although that may be the case. It is, of course, important that the anger and denial be understood. Perhaps another authority figure in the home is the source of intimidation that is reflected in the child drawing. Father? A grandmother? Or, if the patient is an adult man, is he still carrying scars from early conflict with mother? Or has the conflict now become a contemporary one? At work? At home? Does the aggressive mother represent the internalized identification with the aggressor that may provide this individual with his own experience of power to cope with his frightened child-self? The drawings often raise issues for further exploration. And exploring those additional questions immediately allows professionals to move into more depth in evaluations and interpretations.

In children whose object relations are developing in a positive way there is a general progression of age-related developmental stages (see Chapter 4). Children begin at the earliest drawing ages by drawing themselves and mother as almost identical, a sort of mother-and-child "twins," with a somewhat larger size for mother being the only differentiation. As they grow older, the differentiation of figures becomes more complete and individualized. According to Mahler, Pine, and Bergman (1975), the differentiation of the personality of the child from the original symbiotic relationship with the mother normally occurs by the end of the third year. However, in mother-and-child drawings it is not surprising to see the "twinning" style of drawing in 5-year-olds and in immature or regressed 6- or 7-year-olds. Unconscious object representations may remain in an undifferentiated stage longer than external behavior might indicate.

The results of the study described in Chapter 2 suggest that the mother-figure increases in size along with the maturing personality, although the child-figure grows only slightly, suggesting that the "child within" remains exactly that.

Therefore, to see mother-and-child drawings by teens or adults portraying two children is clearly inappropriate and suggests developmental immaturity or regression. This same style of drawing was noted by Schildkrout, Shenker, and Sonnenblick (1972) in their work on adolescent drawings:

> We have been impressed by the large number of drawings that clearly demonstrate an adolescent's image of himself as immature and inadequate. These are drawings that do not show the bizarre qualities of psychosis or the specific anatomical distortions seen in the organically impaired. They are quite simply the portraits of younger children. They do not represent a physical mirror image of a youth, sometimes as old as 18, but rather a psychic inner image reenforced by years of feedback from the significant others in his life who have continued to perceive him as a young child. (p. 22)

Here again the overt evidence in behavior may reflect only dependency of a greater or lesser degree. But the mother-and-child drawing indicates that a closer look should be given to the kinds of dependency and the possibility that those issues are central to the overall personality development. The drawings are particularly useful when they appear in the work of people who present social selves in considerable contrast to the unconscious imagery of the mother-and-child drawings.

Another issue for exploration arises in using the drawings with older adults. The full range of possibilities of internal self and object representations, developed over a lifetime, may be reflected in drawings, from the most to the least mature. However, because most adults have not developed artistic skills, they may be uncomfortable with drawing tasks. It is particularly important that poor drawing ability not exert a penalty.

It is not uncommon for adult women, particularly those who have been most sheltered, to present drawings very much like those of preadolescent girls. When a woman in her fifties draws two little girls with ribbons in their hair for a mother-and-child representation, dependency issues are clearly indicated. Widows and widowers often draw one or both of the figures in a sketchy and/or distorted fashion, as their object relations have had to absorb major loss. The self-image under those circumstances is also often impaired. Serious loss of form typically occurs in degenerative disease, such as Alzheimer's.

It has been said that individuals and families who are happy with themselves and each other are all remarkably similar, but that those who are miserable suffer in highly individual ways. The same may be said of mother-and-child drawings. A positive relationship may be depicted in a number of ways, but there is a similar warm, cheerful-feeling tone to the productions that is independent of artistic ability.

The unhappy portrayals, on the other hand, seem astonishing in their variety and intensity. The impact of the nonverbal communication presented in all the art forms can be at times nearly overwhelming to the viewer, and the mother-and-child representations can add a sense of self and self-with-another that provide a different dimension in assessment and therapy.

CHAPTER 2

Research Issues in Mother-and-Child Drawings

In Chapter 1 some attention is given to validation work with projective drawings, emphasizing the inconclusive nature of the research and often contradictory results of different studies. The projective drawing technique has generated a great deal of interest because of its obvious advantages: It is completely individual, subjective, and creative, avoiding external visual stimuli such as those provided by Rorschach cards; it is nonverbal, thereby avoiding all the cultural issues related to language. In work with young children, it has great appeal as an entertaining activity. It also lends itself to various adaptations related to specific populations, such as the Kinetic-Family-Drawing in family work.

However, clinical psychologists and art therapists tend to have less interest in normative data than do researchers. Art therapists, in particular, typically focus on the highly individual communicative aspects of patient drawings. Psychologists, who have been trained in the use of norms to understand deviance, continue to try to establish one-to-one correspondences between specific drawing characteristics and clinical issues. Some years ago there was considerable hope that a systematic objective scoring system would soon be developed to standardize interpretations of drawings for inclusion in projective test batteries. In an interesting study of values in children (Dennis, 1966), the author commented on the promise of the drawing technique but recognized its limitations. Although commenting on the need for more validation, Dennis offers the following charming analogy:

> We believe that collecting drawings has something in common with collecting plants for an herbarium. The dried and pressed plants are not alive, but they serve usefully in studying the plants which exist in the living world. Drawings can perform a similar service for human psychology. We believe they will prove to be useful, even though they do not provide omniscience. (p. 209)

Since then a number of standardization attempts have been made, addressing a variety of issues.

ARTISTIC QUALITY OF PROJECTIVE DRAWINGS

The issue of the artistic quality of the drawings as influencing the evaluation of the material has been, and remains, a thorny problem. Cressen (1975) compared a patient population with a nonpatient population and found that both psychologists and untrained judges tend to score drawings of high artistic quality as belonging to the nonpatient population and the low art quality drawings as of patient origin. He found that

> very disturbed and regressed individuals often produce obviously bizarre and/or primitive figures. In these cases the quality of the drawing seems to accurately reflect a disorganized mental and emotional state. However, when drawings are not at this extreme, overall quality per se seems to be a much less valid indicator of personality integration. (p. 132)

A large-scale and complex statistical study of three methods of scoring human-figure drawings (Shaffer, Duszynski, & Thomas, 1984) concluded that "most scoring systems merely reflect overall drawing quality" (p. 253). Sims, Dana, and Bolton (1983), in a validation study of the Draw-a-Person as a measure of anxiety, also found drawing quality as a contaminating variable. Feher, Vandecreek, and Teglasi (1983) specifically focused on the issue of art quality in human-figure drawings and found that the problem remained even when the rating clinicians had been warned about such errors.

The variable of art quality may also be expected as a factor in the assessment of mother-and-child drawings. For example, Figure 4.17 may easily be considered a "better" drawing than Figure 4.18 because of its more sophisticated artistic presentation, although the relationship portrayed is much more distant.

DRAWING SIZE

From the earliest attempts to quantify the characteristics of drawings in specific groups, one of the most frequently used measures has been the size of person drawings in various reference groups. Size issues are particularly relevant to mother-and-child drawings because size of person drawings has been assumed to be related to self-esteem ever since Machover's (1949) work. Larger person-figures are associated with assertive personalities and tiny ones, in contrast, with timidity and lack of self-confidence, although extremely large person figures may be associated with grandiosity. Following the same line of interpretation with mother-and-child drawings, it perhaps seems reasonable to consider drawing size as a possible indication of the psychological "size" of the individual in human relationships.

The development of a self-image and the ability to relate to others is generally assumed to be a slightly different psychological process in boys from the parallel process in girls (Freud, 1981; Gedo, 1983). Both boys and girls usually have their first identification with mother, but boys are thought to modify that attachment in order to attain a male self-identity. Girls are assumed to retain the identification with mother longer and to go through a different process in establishing their individuality. (See Chapter 4.)

For all these reasons, some small attempts were made to evaluate the size issue in mother-and-child drawings and to do so by sex in order to evaluate the influences of differences in psychosexual development on drawing size.

Samples of children and adults were obtained within a typical suburban southern California population in which most participants could be considered as enjoying the comfortable middle-class socioeconomic circumstances of the mid-eighties. Most of the participants were White, with a sprinkling of Asians, Hispanics, and Blacks as they happened to occur in public school, church, and community college settings. Total minority representation was less than 15 percent. Harsh living circumstances may have a pronounced effect on the sense of self and relationships, but those issues may be presumed to be minimal in the groups presented here.

Drawings were classified into the following groups:

Group A: Children, ages 6–9
Group B: Preteens, ages 10–12
Group C: Teens, ages 15–18
Group D: Adults

Ages 13 and 14 were omitted because of the fluid state of physical and emotional development during the early adolescent years. The small number of males (n = 12) in the adult sample reflects the difficulty of obtaining "normal" samples in that group; men tend to resist drawing activities. (See comments in Chapters 4 and 5.)

Heights of mother-figures and child-figures were measured in millimeters, and comparisons were drawn within groups by sex.

Tables 1 through 4 present the data comparisons obtained within groups by sex. In most of the groups there were a few drawings that were extremely large in comparison with the rest, tending to skew the statistical results. In order to reduce the influence of those outlying measurements, the data were Winsorized (Dixon & Massey, 1969), a technique that permits the movement of those scores toward the mean for the data analysis. The means and standard deviations were thus modified to reflect more accurately the actual distribution of the majority of the measurements. None of the levels of significance of the t-score comparisons were affected by this procedure.

In the group of young children (Table 1), no statistically significant sex-related differences were obtained in the size of drawings of either figure. In fact, the means of the groups on both mother- and child-figures are almost the same.

TABLE 1
Height Comparisons, Mother- and Child-Figures, by Sex
Group A: Children, Ages 6–9

Drawings	Males [a]		Females [b]		*t*
Mother	*M*	93.75	*M*	93.57	.02 NS
	SD	35.48	*SD*	37.92	
Child	*M*	53.96	*M*	59.82	.71 NS
	SD	22.09	*SD*	32.98	

Note: Mean height measurements are in millimeters.
[a]$n = 24$. [b]$n = 28$

In Table 2 the means of drawing size by the males have dropped precipitously, while the size of the female drawings shows little change. In this preteen group, in contrast to the younger group, the differences between male and female performance are statistically significant.

TABLE 2
Height Comparisons, Mother- and Child-Figures, by Sex
Group B: Preteens, Ages 10–12

Drawings	Males [a]	Females [b]	*t*
Mother	*M* 64.27 *SD* 27.36	*M* 89.66 *SD* 23.98	3.28*
Child	*M* 43.00 *SD* 19.26	*M* 59.34 *SD* 23.66	2.89*

Note: Mean height measurements are in millimeters.
[a]$n = 22$. [b]$n = 21$
*$p = <.01$.

In the teen group (Table 3), there are now marked changes in sample characteristics. Although the differences between the males and females in the size of the mother are still statistically significant, it is perhaps more important to note other changes in the drawings. The drawings of the males have grown in size to resemble those of early childhood, while the drawings of the females have diminished in size.

TABLE 3
Height Comparisons, Mother- and Child- Figures, by Sex
Group C: Teens, Ages 15–18

Drawings	Males [a]	Females [b]	*t*
Mother	*M* 103.13 *SD* 51.89	*F* 81.46 *SD* 33.05	1.71*
Child	*M* 53.26 *SD* 36.52	*F* 45.63 *SD* 24.88	.97NS

Note: Mean height measurements are in millimeters.
[a]$n = 23$. [b]$n = 24$
*$p<.05$.

The adult drawings (Table 4) show yet another major increase in the size of the male drawings of the mother. The female drawings also increase in size, but not so much, and there is now a 25-point statistically significant size difference. In contrast to the large increase in the size of the mother drawings in the male group, the child drawings remained close to the size of the teenage child drawings. The adult females have now increased the size of the child drawings.

Overall, from children through adults, the progression for males, in drawings of the mother figure, shows a major size drop at the preteen age, which is then recovered and increased in the teen group, and further increased in the adult group. For females, the child and preteen group show the size of the mother as larger than those drawn by the males. The

TABLE 4
Height Comparisons, Mother- and Child-Figures, by Sex
Group D: Adults

Drawings	Males [a]	Females [b]	*t*
Mother	*M* 133.33 *SD* 57.96	*M* 101.97 *SD* 48.05	2.12*
Child	*M* 58.41 *SD* 32.59	*M* 60.90 *SD* 29.72	.24 NS

Note: Mean height measurements are in millimeters.
[a]$n = 12$. [b]$n = 28$.
*$p < .05$.

females show a consistent decline in size of drawings from the child to the preteen to the teen groups, with recovery to child level in the adult group. However, the males show a size reduction in mother figures only in the preteen group. Child-figures parallel their mother-figures in size, but they are somewhat larger in the preteen group than they are in the others. In the drawings of teens some of the child figures are presented as babies in arms, and that portrayal increases in the adult group, where nearly all the males show the child either as a baby or small child, usually sitting on the mother's lap.

DISCUSSION

Although the small sample size permits only a few suggestions for further study, there are some interesting trends in the data that go along with the generally held notions about the development of self-concept in males and females.

In the comparisons by sex the young children are relatively equal, with the girls making slightly larger (more confident?) drawings. In the preteen group both groups show a drop in drawing size, but the change is more evident in the work done by the boys. It may be that the drawings in that age group reflect the inhibition of behavior, the learning of rules and self-control, that have traditionally been part of the acculturation process at that age. The drawings suggest that the boys are more seriously affected and that the girls at the same age seem to be experiencing the restrictions as less burdensome.

In the teen groups the boys appear to have regained their male assertiveness, while the girls continue their more controlled and restricted drawing styles, with drawing sizes still smaller than those obtained at preadolescence.

The adult drawings show both groups increasing drawing size, but the drawings by males are now much larger than those of the females.

In relating the findings presented in Tables 1 through 4 to the theoretical notions presented in Chapter 1, it is interesting to speculate about the size of mother- and child-figures in drawings as indicators of basic self-concept issues. First, without reference to the tables, it is obvious that males and females have experienced mothering in ways that are both very similar and very different. Through the developmental years the differences become more apparent and are perhaps reflected in the changes in drawings that can be observed among groups in the tables.

While considering these issues, it is important to remember that the projective nature of the drawings suggests that the portrayals of the mother-figure are not portrayals of the actual mother or mother-substitute. In all age groups, and increasingly so with advances in age, the picture of mother is a representation of an internal object, a psychological reality that derives not only from the original experience of mothering but also from the accretions from other subsequent experiences, both positive and negative, that have affected nurturing.

It is by now a psychological truism that boys receive, at all ages but increasingly so as they grow up, encouragement and active support in their efforts to become effective and powerful. Women typically receive much less of this encouragement, as the now voluminous materials by feminist writers attest (e.g., Gilligan, 1982; Gilligan, Lyons, & Hanmer, 1990; Miller, 1976). No less an authority than Freud (1908/1963), himself a favorite son, commented:

> A well-brought-up woman is, indeed, credited with only a minimum of erotic desire, while a young man has to learn to suppress the overweening self-regard he acquires in the indulgent atmosphere surrounding his childhood. (p. 38)

This sentence carries the implied association of sexuality, indulgence, and self-regard in males only. Although contemporary mores permit women considerably more freedom in sexual behavior than was acceptable in Freud's time, the internal objects of women may not have changed nearly so much, if the results of this study have any validity. The drawings of mother-figures suggest that, for females, loss of assertiveness and self-confidence occur at preteen level and are never completely regained. The drawings by boys suggest that they also lose assertiveness and self-confidence during the latency years, but they regain those characteristics with the teen years and continue to develop them as adults.

The drawings further seem to indicate that the mother-figure grows as the child matures into adulthood, perhaps representing the mature ego and the self who enters into relationships and deals with the external world.

But what of the child drawing? It appears also to develop in tandem with the mother-figure, with its size related to that figure. But it is not subjected to the developmental size changes, either by sex or by age, that appear to affect the mother drawing. However, the actual child drawings are very individual, as are the mother drawings, and there are certainly many defining characteristics other than drawing size that contribute to their value.

As heuristic speculation it is possible to consider the child drawing as representative of the so-called inner child, a construct that was developed by Berne (1961) as an important part of the structure of personality in transactional analysis and more recently developed once again by Bradshaw (1990) in his work with men. It is a concept that rings true at a popular level. The current confessional mode entered with increasing frequency and enthusiasm by celebrities on talk shows and in biographies gives full rein to discussions of extraordinary successes that are seen to be in conflict with an inner childlike sense of inadequacy, fear of punishment, inordinate needs for support, and other issues associated with the earliest years of personality development.

The healthy inner child is mostly compatible with the adult aspects of the personality. It is not often experienced by its possessor, since it is not in conflict and is integrated with the adult personality. A damaged inner child may interfere seriously with the development of the adult personality, remaining almost unchanged even though a false self (Winnicott, 1965) may develop, fostering social and/or economic success. Tentatively, the drawing of the child in the mother-and-child projective drawing may be thought of as yielding some data about the quality of the inner child representation and its relationship to the adult portion of the personality, represented by the mother. In combination, a style of relatedness seems to emerge that may well be central to the experience of self and other that builds the self-concept.

INTERRATER RELIABILITY

The work done thus far has found the group study just described to have a certain utility in identifying trends by age and by sex. It must be emphasized, however, that individual assessment and therapy remains completely individual, and the wide variety of individual responses must be expected, encouraged, and accepted.

This individuality is nowhere so evident as in an attempt to identify pathological drawings as distinct from "normal" ones. Randomly selected drawings by 10 teenage suburban high school males were compared with 10 randomly selected drawings from a group of males incarcerated and identified as psychotic delinquents. Six graduate students in clinical psychology, three male and three female, classified the unidentified drawings as either "normal" or "disturbed." Only one of the raters correctly identified more than 6 of the 10 drawings in each group, and that person identified 7 of the 10.

Then, after considering the possibility that psychology students might not be the best raters of the work of delinquents, a probation officer, a social worker in an inner city area, and a policeman rated the same drawings. The results were the same—each rated 6 of the drawings correctly, but not the same 6. Two of the drawings were flagrantly bizarre and were identified correctly by all raters.

It seems most probable that mother-and-child drawings are of little value in the assignment of individuals to group membership on the basis of drawing characteristics. In that respect mother-and-child drawings differ little from other projective drawing tasks in predictive ability.

Occasionally a truly peculiar drawing will surface in an apparently completely normal setting. Inquiry, where possible, has always thus far elicited explanatory information. For example, a pleasant 12-year-old boy with some reading difficulties produced a drawing with no bodies on the figures and dismembered arms and legs scattered about the page. On inquiry, the boy said he had been recently placed in a foster home, where he was then living, while an apparently endless custody dispute wound itself through the courts. He said that his mother had died the previous year and that he felt "pulled apart" by the conflicting demands of grandparents and two uncles for custody. As the result of the trauma related to his experiences of the previous year, it seemed probable that there was indeed some inner fragmentation of self to go along with his self-perception of being pulled apart. However, the first notion that the drawing was a psychotic one was dispelled.

Some possible formulations have been presented here to give an interpretive schema for mother-and-child drawings. There are no doubt other ways of observing the drawings that may offer other insights and interpretive perspectives. As stated earlier, the drawings examined for this study were all drawn from suburban areas of southern California. Minority cultures are represented only through the accident of their inclusion in some of the groups. Some work, not yet fully developed for publication, has already been done in other countries and other cultures, suggesting important areas for further study.

CONCLUSIONS

The highly personal and idiosyncratic nature of mother-and-child drawings reflects the highly individual nature of human experience. The needs of assessment and treating personnel to find ways of classifying individuals is not a need of the persons to be thus classified, and diagnostic labeling can sometimes interfere with therapy. Although the group classifications of drawings by size (Tables 1, 2, 3, & 4) have yielded interesting information, the comments of Anastasi (1982), suggesting the use of projective drawings only as part of a clinical interview, appear relevant to work with mother-and-child drawings.

CHAPTER 3

The Impact of Art on the Therapist: Transference and Countertransference Issues

Psychological assessments, whether done by psychologists in hospitals, clinics, or schools, are typically done with prescribed test batteries. Projective drawings are often included as required "tests," often with the rationale that they are less costly in time and money than other projective techniques. In many situations they are also considered to require little or no training to administer, since, from this perspective, everyone can look at a drawing and decide whether or not it is a "good" drawing. This rationale has led to a great deal of misuse of projective drawings of all kinds.

Projective drawings are particularly subject to misuse by examiners who have no personal affinity for art. These are the individuals who are always searching for a new "dictionary" of drawings symbols, since the drawings themselves have little communicating power for them.

For many people, art is not important. These individuals do not go to art museums or art shows. They have little or no art in their homes. Freud did not care much for pictorial art, although he enjoyed sculpture (see his response to *Moses* later in this chapter.)

Psychologists, then, may be assumed to have had little or no required participation in art programs as part of their training, in comparison with art therapists, who begin with the advantage of having an art background. On the other hand, most contemporary psychologists have had exposure to object relations concepts and perhaps some introduction to creativity and therapeutic art activities. However, very few professionals have been able to explore the ways in which art impacts on themselves as individuals. Without exploring their own responses to pictorial art, they are at a disadvantage in comprehending how their own issues will appear in countertransference to patient art. New understandings of the importance of transference and countertransference issues in therapeutic settings of all kinds make it extremely important for therapists who have any involvement with patient art to understand something of their own response patterns to pictorial material.

In this fashion perhaps the notion of patient art as something that is evidence of pathology can be expanded to the broader view of artistic nonverbal communication that takes place in every encounter with the work of artists. As psychotherapists learn to observe pieces of art carefully and to wonder about the artists who created them, and then to understand their own responses, their responses to patient material can be extended and enhanced so that both patient and therapist may enjoy more open and empathic communication.

The material in this chapter will discuss mother-and-child art—"real" art, done by artists who have addressed the mother-and-child theme. In this exploration it becomes possible to view pieces of art as communications and to question them—artist intent and viewer response—in ways that are appropriate to patient art as well.

THE MOTHER-AND-CHILD THEME IN ART

The mother-and-child theme in art is a primary one. Not only is Western culture exposed to countless presentations of the Madonna and Child in Christian art of every conceivable style, but nonreligious artists of all periods also turn to the mother-and-child relationship as a favorite subject. That body of work provides indications of the variety of ways in which the mother-child relationship is experienced.

Walk through any art gallery; note the frequency of the mother-child theme and the variations of its expression. Note mothers with babies in arms, sometimes held close in mutual absorption—sometimes held loosely or listlessly in a perfunctory fashion. Toddlers exploring, but not too far from a watchful, smiling mother. Other little ones facing away from a mother absorbed in something or someone else. Note the cool, distant mother-child relationship in one picture and the warmth and intensity of the interaction in another.

A number of artists have explored the theme more than once. Mary Cassatt is probably the best known, for her wonderfully evocative paintings on the mother-child theme.

Henry Moore, who has done a number of powerful mother-and-child pieces, said that a mother-and-child sculpture provides the opportunity to show "the relationship of a large form to a small one, and the dependency of the small form on the larger. Its appeal lies particularly in its expression of two basic human experiences: to be a child and to be a parent" (Fuller, 1987, p. 79).

Picasso has done mother-and-child work in different styles. Which of the Picasso pictures, for example, is the "right" one in its presentation of his notion of the mother-child relationship? It is obvious that the question is an absurdity. However, there is a personality common to those Picasso paintings, often clearly absorbed in technical problems that are understood only by other artists, but often exuberant and carefree, enjoying the mastery of technique and the presentation of content. His mothers seem strong, capable; his infants are large and robust and demanding. Powerful pictures. Now wander over to a Mary Cassatt exhibit and see her bright, sensitive, careful mother-and-child paintings, or to a Gauguin—simple, powerful, restrained in its primitive strength. Even van Gogh has explored the mother-child theme.

The psychological implications of the painting styles have been largely ignored. However, it is the thesis of this chapter that "real" art, like patient art, can be viewed psychologically in two ways: first, for what it says about the artist, and second, for its impact on the viewer.

THE PERSONALITY OF THE ARTIST

Does the painting style represent aspects of the personality of the painter? If a basic definition is accepted of all art as forms of creative self-expression, then the answer appears to be an unarguable "yes." Whether or not the viewer is expected to understand something of the artist's self is another matter. It is a popular notion in some art circles that the artist's work and life are separate; some artists guard their privacy and let their audience know as little as possible about themselves personally. Each piece of art, from that perspective, speaks to each viewer in an individual way, unencumbered by expectations based on the personal qualities of the artist. In psychological terms, the artist invites the projections of the viewer, and the viewer speaks of a personal response to the piece of art. From that perspective, it is irrelevant that Mary Cassatt painted all those wonderful mother-and-child pictures but had no children of her own. But surely no endeavor to understand Mary Cassatt, the person, would ignore her devotion to the depiction of mothers and children.

On the other hand, there are many artists who feel that they want to be understood through their work as expressing their backgrounds and life experiences. Ethnic artists and those interested in making sociological statements are the most obvious examples of this approach. Shows of their work are accompanied by printed materials presenting their backgrounds and the kinds of issues they are exploring. With that kind of information, the viewer's response is materially changed. The individual who painted the picture is now there, to whatever extent the printed material is appropriate and relevant. If the material is poorly chosen and compiled with a prejudicial taint, then the viewer will nevertheless process that information along with the impact of the piece of art itself.

PSYCHOLOGICAL ISSUES IN FORMAL ART

The issue of psychological distress evidenced in formal art is very different. Viewers seldom are aware of personality issues of any kind in artwork, except in the most superficial ways. Some pictures or pieces of sculpture evoke positive responses, and others may be depressing or even horrifying.

The evidences of mental deterioration in van Gogh's work are subject matter in basic art history classes. The well-known and characteristic style of the late van Gogh work is considered the basic example of pathology expressed in art. The loss of structure and the chaotic organization of color evokes an answering sense of chaos in the viewer. Here the artist barely retains control of his medium. In less severely involved individuals, however, various personality issues are less apparent.

But what of other material that seems at least as disorganized to the undiscerning eye? How, then, can therapists arrive at interpretations of patient drawings with more understanding than they bring to the work of artists, who are able to use their talent, training, and skills to convey their meaning without hesitation?

A tentative answer to that question lies in the superior ability of artists to use their skills defensively, to present only what they intend to present, in a style that is their chosen way of communicating themselves to others. Artists make a conscious statement in their work; they know how to create an effect, a response in the observer. Nevertheless, they also express themselves in their choices of subject matter, their styles, and what they avoid. And each artist is distinctively recognizable in the totality of work done over the creative years, as retrospective exhibits clearly show. In this sense, there is a parallel between the work of professional artists and the work of those who draw as part of an evaluation or treatment program. Like professional artists, patients also reveal themselves through their artwork.

PATIENTS AS ARTISTS

Patients are usually not skilled enough in artistic presentation to evoke in treating personnel the kinds of intense response that characterize individual therapist response to, say, Renoir or Francis Bacon. But it seems that they try. It is possible that patients need to hear more about therapist responses to their work, in the fashion that the viewer responds to professional art. Patient art needs to be taken seriously, even during the brief time allotted for assessment, with careful exploration of content and attempts to discern the intent of the communication. Then, by inference, the therapist attempts to explore the internal subjective psychological processes that have evoked a particular expression.

Art therapists know all about the importance of taking the work of their patients seriously at all levels, and that careful attention to the work even of small children is a major part of the strength of their professional activity. Superficial praise, such as the reinforcing "Good girl!" response, reflects a kind of nonresponse that says that no acknowledgment of the small patient-artist's intent has really taken place.

Because assessment personnel are less likely to have had training in art, they are more apt to miss important clues in patient work.

A FREUDIAN EXERCISE IN RESPONSE TO ART

Perhaps the earliest psychoanalytic attempt to explore the impact of an artist's work on the viewer was Freud's (1914/1958)essay on *The Moses of Michelangelo*. Freud, who was himself an avid collector of ancient small sculptural images, acknowledged the "powerful effect" of literature and sculpture on him and his own need to interpret a work of art in order to understand its effect on him. He chose the *Moses* for interpretation, saying, "No piece of statuary has ever made a stronger impression on me than this" (p. 13).

His essay then goes on to become a highly intellectualized analysis of aspects of the positioning of the figure and consideration of the opinions of others who had also attempted to find evidence of the sculptor's intent. Freud followed the usual procedures of his day in art criticism, with the focus on the piece of art and the conscious intent of the artist, rather than on the evocation of the personality and/or subjective concerns of the artist.

However, Freud's original intent to understand the impact of his own experience of the *Moses* is perhaps illuminated in these comments:

> How often have I mounted the steep steps of the unlovely Corso Cavour to the lonely place where the deserted church stands, and have essayed to support the angry scorn of the hero's glance! Sometimes I have crept cautiously out of the half-gloom of the interior as though I myself belonged to the mob upon whom his eye is turned—the mob which can hold fast no conviction, which has neither faith nor patience and which rejoices when it has regained its illusory idols. (p. 14)

These comments provide a vivid glimpse of the inner Freud, a powerful man confronted with a powerful sculpture of perhaps the most formidable character in his own personal Jewish heritage. Everything known about Freud emphasizes his strong personal power and his efforts to maintain that power in an often disparaging professional community. He certainly held fast to his convictions and spent his life in attempts to root out the "illusory idols" that he saw all around him. Without going into the issues of faith and patience in his life, it remains easy to see why it was important to him to be able to try to look Moses in the eye and stand up to the "angry scorn" that he found there. His own sense of not measuring up to heroic standards seems to have been evoked in a humbling experience that was a typically sensitive response of the Jewish intellectuals of the time.

Contemporary approaches to this material might conclude that Freud worked out his intellectual analytic essay as a means of gaining control and establishing his power over the disturbing sculpture. This essay yields an inadvertent glimpse of the importance of the power issue in his life and his style of mastering anxiety-producing material—he used the power of his intellect to transform the material into cognitive issues that he then dealt with conceptually.

The Freudian response to the *Moses* of Michelangelo illustrates the important point that viewing a work of art often evokes in the viewer responses that reveal psychological processes at work. When this response occurs in a therapist in response to patient work, the event is considered a countertransference phenomenon.

On the other hand, the interpretation can be moved in the other direction, to view evidences of personal issues in the lives of artists as presented in their work. For example, there have been a number of studies of Michelangelo's life that have described his care by a wet-nurse for his first two years and his mother's death when he was 6 as interrupting the bonding with his mother. His presentation of female figures in painting and sculpture is notably remote and uninvolved.

Works of art that reflect the mother-and-child theme evoke specific responses from observers. The observations and interpretations presented here are the personal ones of the author and presumably are not always—or perhaps even often—the ones that will be evoked in others. After all, each individual brings personal interests and issues to an art gallery as well as to patient work. But it is important that each therapist become sensitive to his or her own individual internal response styles. In so doing, the therapist develops the ability to work effectively with patient art material, just as that same type of sensitivity to the oral communication of patients enhances the power of the spoken therapeutic interaction.

BOOKS ON MOTHER AND CHILD IN ART

It is perhaps important here to draw attention to three major books that provide selections of famous mother-and-child art and interpretive commentary and/or viewer response. The earliest, *Mother and Child*, a book compiled by Lawrence (1975) and now unfortunately out of print, contains wonderful reproductions of 100 works of art on the mother-child theme, with comments by "distinguished people" who chose them as favorites. The commentary provided by such diverse celebrities as Donna Reed, Fleur Cowles, Anäis Nin, Joshua Logan, Oleg Cassini, and Princess Grace of Monaco, as well as J. Paul Getty and Norton Simon (both respected as informed appreciators of art), is wonderful in its diversity and rich in insights into each collector's point of view.

A second book on the mother-and-child theme is *Art of Motherhood*, by Tobey (1991), which contains a wealth of outstanding photos of pieces of art and warm, informed commentary. This book focuses on "a variety of experiences of motherhood" through a number of ages and cultures. Tobey makes a point of her own pregnancy paralleling the development of the book, a circumstance that appears to add the richness of her personal involvement to the intellectual endeavor.

Another recent book is Langer's *Mother and Child in Art* (1992), a book filled with huge and glorious photos, and also numerous details from the art she has chosen to photograph. The book is an engrossing celebration of mothers and children done by a feminist art critic, author, and lecturer. She also incorporates object relations understandings in her commentary:

> The infant comes to define itself by internalizing the most momentous aspects of the relationship which will inform his or her understanding of the self and the world, the emotions, and the ability to love the self and others. The growing child's psychic structure and sense of reality—issues of intimacy and identification—are defined by how he or she recreates these experiences in adulthood. So the infant's actual relationship with the mother and the feelings about her remain influential throughout life. (p. 7)

Langer includes much useful comment on the lives of the artists and the circumstances of the works of art, helping the viewer to interpret the material in light of the artist's intent. She describes Claude Monet's *Woman with a Parasol—Madame Monet and Her Son* (Figure 3.1):

> Monet's relationship with Camille was a troubled one....Unlike his mother, Jean [the son] faces the viewer directly, staring out as though trying to connect with someone who can offer him the solace that he is unable to get from his distracted parent. In this composition Monet expresses the feelings of estrangement that he himself often felt when he observed Camille's relationship with her son. (p. 111)

Monet did another painting of Jean as an infant in his crib. In that initial picture, the baby occupies the position of interest, while Camille is facing away toward the baby. Only the back of her head is visible to the viewer. But by the time of this later painting, Jean is now pushed into the background.

From the perspective of this book, it might also be useful to consider the position of Jean in this later painting as Monet's position in his own early relationship with his mother. If so, then the mother-and-child painting presumably reflects a personal sense of alienation from self and others, which may have contributed to Monet's notoriously difficult relationship with Camille during the course of their marriage.

Each of the three books described is developed from the author's own perspective on the mother-and-child relationship; each contributes

Figure 3.1. Claude Monet, *Woman with a Parasol—Madame Monet and Her Son* (Collection of Mr. and Mrs. Paul Mellon, © 1993 National Gallery of Art, Washington, D.C.).

something of the author to the final product. In the Lawrence book, Mary Lawrence is listed as the "compiler," and she has abdicated her own voice to the voices of those who chose and commented on the works of art. The other two books contain much more of the authors. It is particularly interesting to compare the commentary of the Tobey and Langer books when they discuss the same pieces.

FOCUS ON ART

Mother-and-child art may be organized in a number of ways. For a general focus, which also has relevance to patient drawings, the following artwork will be categorized into material that focuses primarily (1) on the child, (2) on the mother, and (3) on the relationship between the two. In the choice of artwork for inclusion in this chapter, considerations have been devoted primarily to work that illustrates a point concerning mother-child relationships. Portrait work has been avoided, for the most part, since the effort to produce a likeness tends to limit the projections in the material. The exception is the wonderfully personal and expressive self-and-mother picture done by Arshile Gorky (see Figure 3.7).

Even the recognition that a particular work is done based on the posing of a particular model does not alter these circumstances. Models are used for a number of reasons, but the model is seldom considered the subject of a nonportrait piece of art.

Some of the art pieces discussed in this chapter are from the world's acknowledged greatest art. Others are done by serious contemporary artists. Still others are decorative or commercial art, reproduced in quantity and sold in gift shops. No matter. Something of the artist appears in the portrayals. However, that "something" is also subject to reinterpretation as the result of the viewer's own projections into the work. Here I hope the reader will find a good deal of enjoyment in noting areas of disagreement with my interpretations. I hope the areas of disagreement will also evoke a desire in the reader to identify personal projections into the material, and will lead to increased sensitivity to the many issues involved in the understanding of the art productions of others.

Focus on the Child

In many of the pieces of art following the mother-and-child theme the center of the piece and the focus of attention is clearly the child. In these situations the mother is seen in a supporting role.

The countless Madonna and Child paintings produced over the centuries sometimes focus on the Holy Child and sometimes on the Mother of God. Most of them are, for that reason, very serious in tone. There are a few noted exceptions celebrating the humanness of the Jesus and Mary figures. Wood's (1992) *The Nativity* presents an amazing number of types and styles of Madonna and Child paintings.

The little-known *Madonna and Child* painting by Antonello da Messina (Figure 3.2) is a perfect example of a work focused on the child. The figure of Mary is supportive of the child, but her calm smile and downcast gaze forms a backdrop for the very active infant Jesus, who looks out of the picture, engaging the viewer, as he puts his hand into the neckline of his mother's dress, with just the faintest suggestion that he is reaching, as babies so often do, for his mother's breast. The intimacy of this portrayed relationship reflects the interior freedom of the artist and the cultural approval that allowed artists of the time considerable freedom of expression.

Focus on the Mother

Today, the perception of "mother" is that of a parent, defined in a role by the child she parents. "Mother," as a concept, has been to some extent divorced from the concept of "woman." It has not always been so. Art, philosophy, and psychology have all contributed extensive work on varying images of motherhood. The internal images of mother have been discussed not only in the object relations literature but also in the Jungian literature on archetypes. A comprehensive treatment of the "great mother" archetype was done by Erich Neumann (1955/1963). From the object relations point of view, it is interesting to note how few of the art pieces reproduced in this book contain children.

The "great mother," says Neumann, is "an inward image at work in the human psyche," whose symbolic expression is found in "the myths and artistic creations of mankind" (p. 3). As such, it includes the "feminine" images, as well as fertility goddesses. In this perspective the mother is equivalent to an internal notion of the female in all her manifestations. Therefore, this "mother" can exist without a child. She is not a parent figure but something much more elemental.

Figure 3.3 is a more sophisticated treatment of the theme, done by an artist from Uganda who recalls watching his young brother being tossed in the air with joy by his mother when he was very small. The wonderful freedom represented by this work, which is a print of a Paul Nzalamba batik original in rich color, appears to reflect the maternal permission that allowed him to leave his home and find success as an artist in the United States. Along with the freedom, note the security

Figure 3.2. Antonello da Messina, *Madonna and Child* (Andrew W. Mellon Collection, © 1993 National Gallery of Art, Washington, D.C.).

Figure 3.3. Paul Nzalamba, *At Play* (Courtesy of the artist, © 1989 Paul Nzalamba, Los Angeles, California). Photographed by Carl J. Thome.

represented by the huge feet, so well grounded to provide safety for the growing, exploring child.

Focus on the Relationship

Most mother-and-child art places its focus on the relationship, giving each figure importance and portraying something about the interaction (or lack of it) that affects them both.

Figure 3.4 is an unusual and contemporary Madonna and Child in which both the Holy Child and Mother have equal importance. In an intensely human and vibrant portrayal, a young, happy, teenage Madonna delights in her infant, who mirrors and responds with his own reciprocal pleasure. There is real joy in this painting and in the many other mother-and-child paintings and sculptures done by Juan Ferràndiz, a Spanish artist and poet. Concerning childhood, he says,

> Childhood is not only a stage of life to leave, but the child is the root that allows the man to be alive. To believe in the child is to believe in oneself....To keep the child is an essential condition for man to feel himself. (J. Ferràndiz I Castells, personal communication, October 12, 1992)

The work of Ferràndiz suggests that he has indeed been able to keep his own inner child very much alive and nurtured.

Ted De Grazia's *Mother and Child* (Figure 3.5) is a figurine by a well-known Southwestern artist. In this piece the mother has no facial features and is turned away from the child, whose eyes are closed. The very popular De Grazia figures, which often appear in his paintings, notecards, and sculptures, are very much alike from piece to piece and often have blank faces. In this one the child with closed eyes (preoccupied with inner fantasies?) stands next to the mother, who holds her close in a shared tactile communion. The deliberate omission of the features on the faces appears in this instance to invite the viewer's projections and identifications.

Another mother-and-child figure in which the mother and the child have nearly identical faces is Figure 3.6. This Schmid music box plays *Love Makes the World Go Round*, and the old-fashioned clothing, the girl carrying her doll, and the girl's clothing as a youngster's version of her mother's gown all reflect a time when it was taken for granted that a young girl was to learn to be just like mother. That kind of imitation carries a culture from one generation to the next with a minimum of disruption. However, it is disturbing to see how little the figures differ and how little room for individuality is permitted in the relationship

Figure 3.4. Juan Ferràndiz, *Madonna and Child* (Courtesy of the artist, Juan Ferràndiz, Barcelona, Spain). Photographed by Carl J. Thome.

Figure 3.5. Ted De Grazia, *Mother and Child* (Courtesy De Grazia Foundation, © 1990 De Grazia Foundation, Tucson, Arizona).

Figure 3.6. Music box, *Love Makes the World Go Round* (© Schmid 1981). Photographed by Carl J. Thome.

portrayed here. The idealized traditional role of women in American society is clearly visible here, with all its charm, safety, and limitations.

Arshile Gorky's painting (Figure 3.7), done in muted but carefully chosen colors, is a particularly unusual one. Gorky was a gifted but deeply troubled artist who never surmounted the turmoil and grief of his early years in Armenia. This picture looks like the work of a severely depressed individual. Gorky's mother died when he was still in his teens in Armenia, and his sense of responsibility for her never left him. In this painting the mother is in front, staring implacably out at the viewer, giving no sense that she will respond favorably to the entreaties of her son, who is trying to approach with his floral offering. Note the ambivalence expressed in the body turned toward the mother, but with the legs and feet turned the other way to take him out of the picture. A close, symbiotic tie is suggested in the similarity of features and expressions of the two figures. The intense eye emphasis recalls the eyes in the Monet painting of Jean. It is interesting to compare Gorky's painting with Figure 4.20, where a boy tries to cope with an overwhelming mother whose large, empty figure dominates the picture.

No, Figure 3.8 is not a patient painting. However, the stark aggression of those teeth in mother's wide smile and the intent, staring gaze of both figures give the viewer pause. This fascinating painting shows the way in which a professional artist can project the pain of intense personal loss into a direct portrayal in a piece of art. Says Alan Kirk (through L. Hedges, personal communication, July 10, 1992),

> The picture emerged suddenly from some unknown place inside and was painted rapidly. Only a few weeks later my lover of twelve years (Nick Cornwell, also an artist) died suddenly and unexpectedly from an undiagnosed HIV infection. My unconscious must have been aware that once again I was being abandoned. I was given up for adoption not long after birth and abandoned again some years later by my stepmother. Nick's impending illness and death must have called forth this deep image.

Amid a wealth of fascinating detail, it is perhaps most important to note the lack of the top of the head (the brain or thinking part) on each figure. The sleeve of the mother's dress shows in the empty space between the eyes on the infant, and what appears to be hair on the mother's head also seems to be mountains in the background. The mother's head, like the child's, lacks its rational component. What a wonderful image to express the *mindless* primitive fury that spills forth in this painting, uninhibited by cognitive mediation!

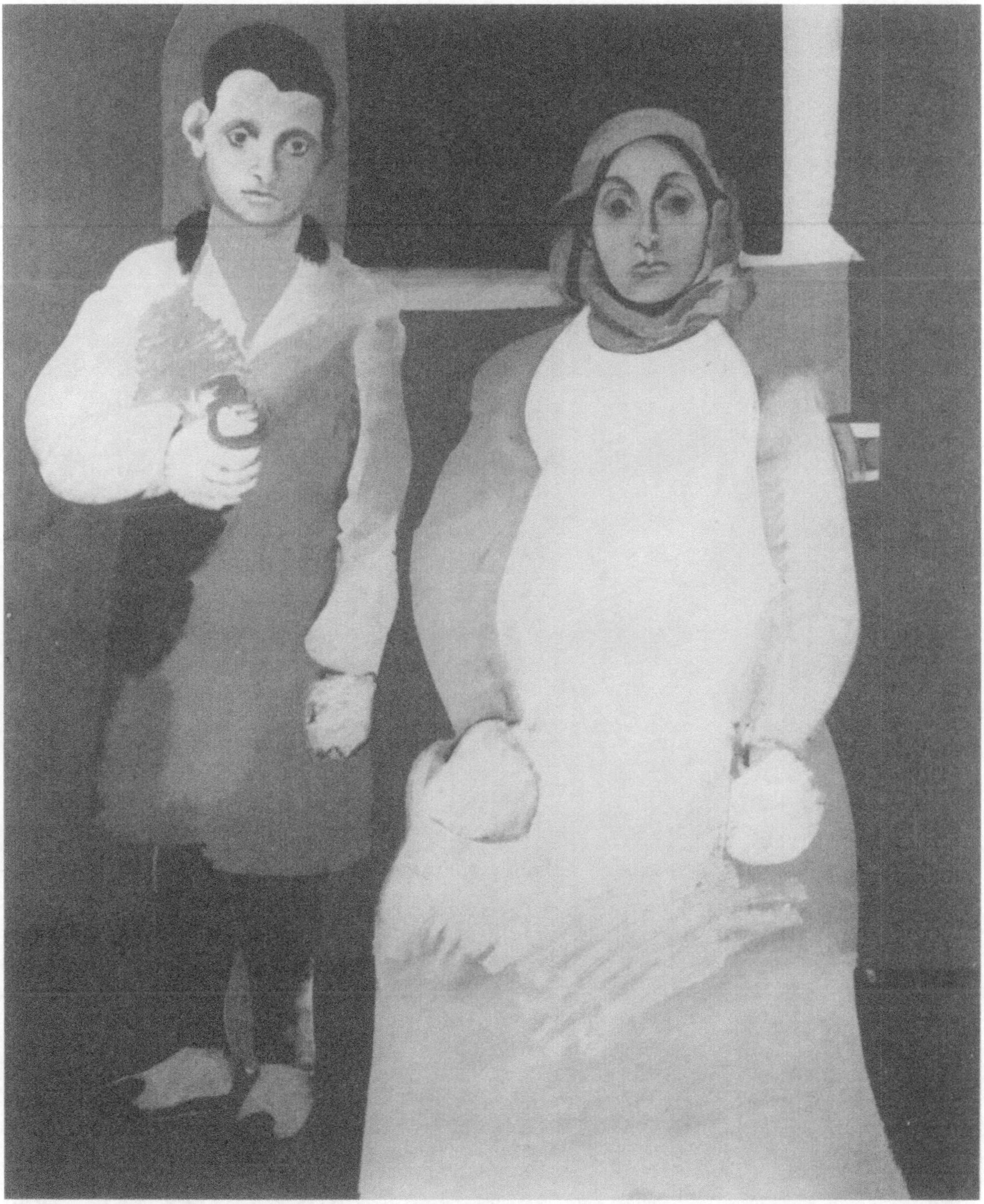

Figure 3.7. Arshile Gorky, *The Artist and His Mother* (ca. 1926–1936, Oil on canvas, 60 x 50 in. [152.4 x 127 cm.], 50.17; Collection of Whitney Museum of American Art, New York; Gift of Julien Levy for Maro and Natasha Gorky in memory of their father).

Figure 3.8. Alan Kirk, *Mother and Child with Teeth* (Courtesy L.E. Hedges, Orange, California).

It is important to note here that under the intense pressure of grief the artist has not only moved into his own unconscious processes but has also chosen the mother-and-child image, that most primitive internal representation of relatedness, as the vehicle for his self-expression. This amazing painting serves as a reminder that the central core of intense unconscious feeling is fundamental to the human experience, usually unknown except in times of overwhelming stress.

The Kirk painting, with its graphic power enhanced by the use of intense colors, perfectly exemplifies the ways in which artistic fluency permits the kind of expression on the part of the professional artist that is not available to most patients in therapy. However, viewing work like Kirk's is a fine preparation for the therapist who must attempt to understand a number of ways in which patients present their own issues.

CHAPTER 4

Administering and Interpreting Mother-and-Child Drawings: A Developmental Perspective

GENERAL CONSIDERATIONS

The use of mother-and-child drawings as a projective technique rests on the theoretical assumptions of object relations theory and the work of ego and self psychologists, who place specific emphasis on the crucial importance of the earliest and most fundamental of interpersonal relationships, that between a mother and her child. Because of its primacy and intensity, this relationship is considered to have a peculiarly important role in the emotional development of the child.

The kind of relating established in that early setting provides a subjective pattern, or a set of expectations, that continues to function in subsequent relationships. Gradually, through the accretions of experience, the mother of early experience becomes a sort of abstraction, a theoretical construct of "mother" that includes other experiences of nurturing and lack of nurture that affect the internal sense of self and others. Mother-and-child drawings, therefore, should reflect a particular mode of relating to others that may prove clinically rewarding.

The approach to interpretation of mother-and-child drawings presented here represents an adherence to a psychodynamic view of personality development, with notions about merger, separation, and individuation issues and the existence of unconscious content in drawings that may prove uncongenial to behaviorally oriented professionals. However, I will also discuss dependency and developmental issues as they appear in the drawings from a more general clinical perspective. The following comments attempt a clinical outlook with applications suitable to a variety of theoretical and professional views. Other interpretations will occur to the reader, no doubt, since the subjective and individual nature of the interpretations is second only to the subjectivity and individuality of the drawings themselves.

Like dreams, drawings are completely individual and personal. Both have wide current acceptance in various forms of psychotherapy. Dreams may reflect current issues in an individual's life. But dreams also present material influenced by unconscious themes and motives, thereby offering Freud's "royal road to the unconscious" for scrutiny during the psychotherapeutic hour. Seen as communication, drawings also present something of the self to the receptive other, carrying both conscious manifest content and also other aspects of being that are nonverbal and not immediately accessible to conscious cognitive understanding.

Being understood is a powerful experience, and the sense of being understood through graphic expression has been a strong motivator for professional artists. That same motivation leads art students, as well as patients in art therapy, to convey pictorially something of themselves to others in order to be understood.

Exactly what any individual is willing to risk in presentation at any given time is clearly the reflection not only of an inner state but also of the situation that is calling up the material. The difference between the kinds of drawings evoked in a psychological assessment procedure and those produced in art therapy have often led to heated debate as to which presentations are the "right" ones, as if contradictory communications are issues to be resolved rather than understood and appreciated in the context of their creation.

It is important to consider that art therapy patients or others going through assessment procedures are usually wary about their self-expression, since often they are in a position to receive negative or even punitive consequences from self-revelation, such as hospitalization or restriction of their activities. Custody arrangements and educational placements often ride on the results of assessment of children, and the child who knows this can be very apprehensive indeed. Defensiveness and a certain constriction is therefore not at all unusual for individuals undergoing psychological assessment and must be considered appropriate.

The same constraints seldom exist in art therapy situations, which tend to be part of a total ongoing treatment process and often one of the most enjoyable aspects of the treatment. In such cases the art therapist has a chance to establish a warm and trusting relationship in which freedom of expression is easy and the desire to communicate the self evolves through the course of therapy. The nature of the personal "story" obtained in this manner can be rich indeed, as many collections of drawings or other art obtained through the course of treatment can dramatically attest.

INSTRUCTIONS FOR DRAWINGS

It is important that whatever a person produces in the way of a mother-and-child drawing be simply accepted, without either disapproval or effusive delight. Psychologists experienced in clinical assessment learn to focus on the material presented either verbally or in other ways with careful but nonjudgmental interest and attention in an attempt to understand it as fully as possible.

The standard 8½-by-11-inch sheet of paper is presented the usual vertical way. However, if the individual chooses to turn the page horizontally, that should be accepted. In person drawings the paper orientation is sometimes considered significant, but in mother-and-child drawings a horizontal placement is often chosen in order to frame the two figures evenly.

The instructions for both sexes and all ages are simple—*"Draw a mother and child."* Note that the instructions do *not* ask for *your* mother, or for a mother and *her* child, or a mother and *a* child. Apparently, these small differences tend to alter the focus of the individual who is establishing a mental set for the drawing task. The history of the culture in the West has established an abstract sense of the mother-child relationship that seems to be reflected in the "mother-and-child" phrase. It is repeated over and over in Christian religious art, along with the phrase "Madonna and Child," for which it is often a variant. It has also become included in various secular presentations of a concept of the mother-child relationship so that it seems to have a meaning at a conceptual level that requires little further explanation. Each approach to the task is completely individual and seems to reflect both the universality and the specialness of the mother-child relationship.

Although teens and adults typically have no difficulty in responding to the instructions in abstract terms, a child will often ask, "My mother?" which immediately suggests that the distinction is already being drawn between "my" mother and a generalized abstraction of "mother" as a concept. Other children, who have not yet drawn that distinction, immediately proceed to draw their own mothers, as their comments during the drawing often indicate. There is no problem in this task approach—it simply reflects the individual's conceptual organization of the mother-child relationship, which is still personal and specific. Those with intellectual impairments also typically draw "my mother," since the concrete aspects of their thinking lead them in that direction. The projective aspects of the drawings, of course, are the inclusion of aspects of the personal mother-child relationship within the more abstract formulation.

From the teenage years, the mother figure takes on a more contemporary appearance. The question "My mother?" is heard very seldom and suggests continued childlike dependency or lack of ability to abstract.

To return to the child's question: The examiner's response should be nondirective. Repeat the instructions; perhaps add, "Just a mother-and-child," or "However you wish to do it." Sometimes there is the question, "Does it have to be human?" Keep to the nondirective format. Some remarkable drawings have been produced of nonhuman representations of the relationship.

GUIDELINES FOR INTERPRETATION OF DRAWINGS

Ever since the original use of projective drawings as a psychological tool for the exploration of personality and emotional issues (Machover, 1949), there has been little disagreement that in some fashion or other the artistic productions of self-figures, family-figures, and a wide range of other pictorial presentations of aspects of individual experience communicate aspects of the self. However, since the use of drawings has met with such a variety of results and since there have been almost as many studies questioning the utility of drawings as a projective device as there have been supporting their use, it seems wise to establish rather clearly the limits of the kinds of interpretations that can legitimately be made from mother-and-child drawings.

First, it seems important to emphasize that mother-and-child drawings, like other personal drawings, partake of a mixture of current moods, recent experiences, and long-term, stable personality characteristics.

The interpretive guidelines presented here will, therefore, focus on the modes of relating as they may be expressed in the drawings. Relating styles may be temporary, partial, or characterological. They may also express one aspect of conflicted feelings.

Finally, it is necessary to emphasize that indications of personal characteristics or pathology suggested by drawings should be considered as just that—indications for further assessment, confirmation, or rejection. Drawings also reflect sociocultural circumstances and values that must be considered in their interpretation. Clinicians are warned often enough about overinterpretation of data, but it still seems important to reiterate the usual cautions about reading too much into drawings and, in particular, to avoid cookbook-style interpretations of pictorial detail without adequate supporting evidence. No conclusions should ever be drawn on the basis of drawings alone, just as all indicators of pathology or personal characteristics obtained in any form of assessment procedure should be subject to cross validation through multiple measures.

With all these cautions in mind, it becomes possible to turn to some general characteristics that seem to appear regularly in this small task that may tell something about an individual's perception of the most important relationship in early life—and the prototype of later relationships.

DEVELOPMENTAL CONSIDERATIONS

At all ages, given the limitations of developmental ability to draw, the relationship between the mother and child figures should be reasonably close (approximately within touching distance, if an arm were to be extended) and present either two figures side by side or a mother clearly holding or caring for a child. This style of drawing appears typical at all age levels. Young children tend to draw the mother-and-child figures as much alike, side by side, and in child proportions, with large, childlike heads. More adult proportions are typical in the drawings of teenagers and adults, who also tend to portray more often the mother in the caring role. The mother-figure becomes more adult as the developmental age increases.

The following drawings vary widely in drawing style and artistic proficiency. They are arranged to provide representative samples of age-typical drawings and to provide an indication of the wide variety of expressive drawing styles that exist among individuals at similar developmental stages. Each can be considered a specific communication.

The drawings in this chapter have been selected from many hundreds of drawings. Most of the child drawings were obtained in schools, either individually or in groups. Some were obtained in church groups, as were many of the adult drawings. None of these drawings were obtained in patient populations or special groups (such as special education groups in schools), which might be expected to present atypical material. Drawings obtained from various groups with demonstrated pathologies or developmental abnormalities are shown in Chapter 5. Here, it is important to obtain an idea of the usual developmental sequence of drawing characteristics from early childhood through the adult years—the gradual addition of detail and change of form and style of the figures.

Although children begin to draw at an early age, representational drawing (drawing a likeness of a mental representation, rather than exploring line and color) is usually developed by the age of 5 and reinforced by kindergarten exercises in drawing (Kellogg, 1967). The ability to draw human figures with some facility is usually fairly well established by age 6. At that age the manipulation of a pencil and the exploration of basic shapes has typically been mastered.

As the child grows and develops, a parallel development becomes apparent in drawing techniques. Those developmental factors appear in mother-and-child drawings in more differentiated and well-detailed figures. However, those increasing skills in drawing are used in the service of self-expression and do not, in themselves, produce drawings reflecting mature self-representations and relationships. The child's self-perception and sense of relationships with others is portrayed as it exists at the current level of psychological development.

Mother-and-child drawings reflect all kinds of self-perceptions and perceptions of others. Some of those perceptions are overt and easy to understand. Others seem less accessible. They change over time and respond to specific stresses. But, as in other representations of the self, there is usually a kind of core consistency to a drawing style that reflects the individual personality. In the work of professional artists, for example, styles may evolve and grow, but a retrospective exhibition is typically devoted to following the developmental process of a particular artist. It is not unreasonable to anticipate the same kinds of consistency in less proficient artistry. In fact, individual drawing styles are apparent in every primary school class and in ongoing art therapy groups, just as "real" artists have work that is easily recognizable. In turn, we may postulate some sort of ongoing consistency of notions of the self and others that remains central to the personality and that comes forth in artistic expression.

The drawings presented here in age sequence reflect a wide variety of perceptions of the mother-child relationship, many of which may be readily understood. Some present generally positive relationships;

others may be less so. It is the work of projective interpretation to suggest that those presentations also have significance for understanding something of the self that may not be explicit, conscious, or cognitively understood.

DEVELOPMENTAL DRAWINGS

Drawings by Young Children

Young children usually draw mothers and children as very much alike, usually side by side and perhaps touching hands. That particular style of drawing appears to retain elements of the early sense of mother-and-child oneness, or the early symbiotic relationship between mother and child. As the child forms a separate and individual identity, that identity is reflected in increasing differentiation between the mother- and child-figures in the child's drawings. That separation is an individual matter and reflects a whole constellation of factors in the child's development.

Figure 4.1, done by a boy age 6.6 (6 years and 6 months), shows well-developed figures with strength and a sense of cheerful self-confidence. The figures look a great deal alike but size differentiation is occurring.

In contrast, Figure 4.2 is a drawing that appears quite immature, even for a little boy just turning 6. Note the total absence of a body, with legs descending from the head to form a sort of body outline. The circle within the mother's body area suggests either a hole or a baby within. Is that a penis next to that hole? This little boy may have some anxieties about mother's body, babies in mothers, and sex that make it difficult for him to deal with bodies just now. Is mother pregnant? Is she seen as sexually aggressive? Although there may well be a benign developmental situation here, the possibility of penetration and molestation associated with that hole in the mother figure's body and lack of body shape need to be considered. Remember that the possible molestation could have occurred to the child but could have been projected onto the mother-figure in the drawing. In mother-and-child drawings, children typically identify with the child-figure, of course, but unacceptable parts of the self-identification may be presented in the mother-figure. For example, an obese child may draw the child-figure at normal weight but draw a huge mother although the actual mother may be quite thin.

Note that the figures in this drawing are farther apart than usual, perhaps reflecting avoidance, rejection, or even protective distance. The presence of hair on the child's head, even though there is very little detail of any kind in the picture, suggests reoccupation with hair, perhaps as strength or, again, some sort of sexual concern.

Figure 4.1. Male, age 6.6

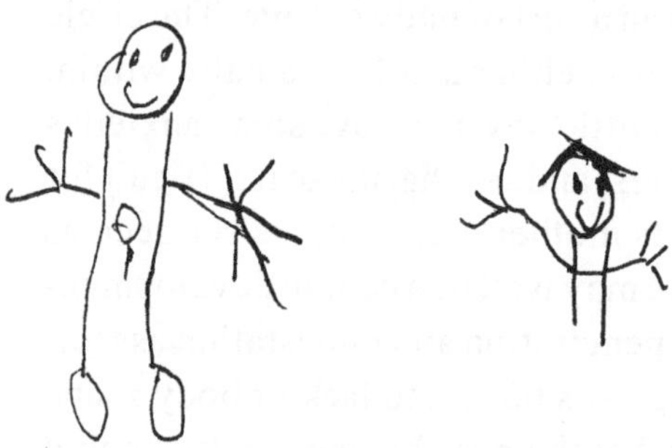

Figure 4.2. Male, age 6.1

Figure 4.3, by a girl, age 6.4, presents very large figures whose apparent self-confidence is belied by the absence of hands on both figures and feet on the mother. Note the similarities of these figures. The shading on the child's arms suggests some anxiety about reaching out assertively, and the lack of both feet and hands on the mother gives the impression that this child does not yet have a well-developed sense of control or security. A child experiences personal strength partly through experiencing the security and strength of the parent.

Figure 4.4 is by a girl the same age as the one who drew Figure 4.3, but this drawing is less well-developed. Mental age here may be the factor. In fact, amount and appropriateness of detail should always be considered in terms of overall developmental level, since paucity of detail may simply reflect some developmental delays or limitations in general mental ability (Harris, 1963).

Although Figure 4.5 was drawn by a girl a bit younger than the ones who did the preceding drawings, the maturity level is much higher. The mother and child are clearly differentiated. However, the separation may have come at a heavy price. The mother is presented as extremely dominating, with aggressive-looking and possibly dangerous hands and the child floating helplessly at her side. These feelings may be transient and situation-specific, or they may be pervasive and longstanding. The child may never have been able to form a close early relationship with a hostile and rejecting mother.

Mother's hand overlapping the tree may suggest her relation to the father, and it is not clear if the bird (self) is flying toward or away from the alliance.

Figure 4.6 was done by a 7-year-old girl, who, in spite of limited drawing skills, fairly radiates energy, and the huge arms on the child seem quite aggressive. However, the child-figure originally had tiny, helpless-looking arms held close to the body. Perhaps linking with mother increases her sense of power. Are the figures well grounded, or are they clinging to the ground for support and security?

By age 8, female children use more detail in their drawings and mothers are drawn in more adult proportions. We can see this in Figure 4.7, where mother and daughter are still very similar, and mother wears a hair ribbon, but the mother is much larger and truer to adult proportions. (See Chapter 3 for comments on figure size.)

Mother's eyes are completed with pupils, while the child's remain blank, which suggests that mother is perceived as both larger in physical size and greater in her ability to "see" her way in the world. The two are represented in relation to a tree and a flower. The tree is small and much lighter in line emphasis than either of the person drawings, suggesting

Figure 4.3. Female, age 6.4

Figure 4.4. Female, age 6.4

Figure 4.5. Female, age 6.2

Figure 4.6. Female, age 7

Figure 4.7. Female, age 8

the fragility of the inner self that we see in the child drawing and in the similarities in the mother-and-child figures. However, the relatively large and assertive flower suggests growth.

Girls often mature in drawing skills, as well as in other eye-hand coordination abilities, earlier than age-peer boys. Figure 4.8, for example, is the work of an 8-year-old boy. The figures are quite crude and little detail is offered. Note the similarity of stance and body structure of the figures and the considerable distance between the two. These figures are somewhat impoverished and may reflect either actual emotional impoverishment and/or distance or constriction of emotional expression. Cultural attitudes toward boys and their self-expression often serve to limit their freedom in creative activities.

Drawings at Preadolescence

Preadolescence has often been described as the calm before the storm of adolescence, the traditional latency period of avoidance of intense feelings and development of self-control and stronger ego functions.

Figure 4.8. Male, age 8

Teen social concerns increasingly affect this age group; nevertheless, some of the drawings in this group reflect the traditional developmental concerns. Others are all too clearly involved in the adolescent struggle. Size of the mother tends to decrease in this age group as the child's psychological size increases.

Figure 4.9 was drawn by a 12-year-old boy. Note the proportions here, where the mother and child are appropriately different in size and proportion. Note also the warm relationship between the two, established by the smiles and eye contact. This young man seems to be clinging to the protection of the little boy role as yet, not unusual in preteens, when an early closeness is reactivated before the adolescent separation. However, the breasts on mother suggest a growing awareness of sexual characteristics.

Figure 4.10 is another drawing by a boy, age 11, who is already having a try at adult male self-assertion. Mother is still larger than the child, and she still shares head style and facial features with the child. However, the "son," carefully and emphatically labeled, has a burgeoning muscle in his arm, and he is trying to get a grip on a phallic gun,

Figure 4.9. Male, age 12

Figure 4.10. Male, age 11

aimed in a direction away from mother. Perhaps he is unconsciously denying aggression toward mother, or expressing a sexual-aggressive aim elsewhere.

Figure 4.11 shows yet another way that an 11-year-old male deals with the same issue. In this picture mother remains the nurturer, providing the child with a snack. The child has his arms out. Note the heavy shading, however, which raises some questions about the mother's style of giving to the boy. Note the careful desexualization of both figures, along with the indirect sexuality in the crotch emphasis, pockets, and the anxious sexualization in the heavy shading of mother's large feet.

There is a kind of rigid immobility in this drawing that suggests a youngster still caught up in a dependency on mother that he is not yet able to challenge. At age 11 this cannot be considered as other than normal, but a similar drawing obtained from a young adult male would suggest developmental arrest in identify formation.

Now we have a girl's approach to the same issues in Figure 4.12. This 11-year-old girl is clearly in an intense dependency on her mother, and this dependency contains a good deal of idealization. Note not only the girl's admiring gaze but also the sun shining in the corner of the picture. Suns are ubiquitous in the drawings of young children, perhaps as internalized symbols of maternal warmth, but are seldom found in the work of older children and adults.

Figure 4.11. Male, age 11

Figure 4.12. Female, age 11

Proportions are well-defined, and the drawing is firm. Heavy hair shading, belt emphasis, and mother's purse seem once again to reflect the sexual issues that confront adolescents and are the only indications as yet of the struggle for separation and adult sexual identity that will be forthcoming in the next years.

In another drawing by an 11-year-old girl (Figure 4.13), we see that she is more overtly into the struggle for the female role. Her present solution is to put herself first and to make herself into a copy of mother, including makeup. The garments are similar; however, the mother's shape is modified just enough to allow mother sexuality but not yet herself. The heightened similarity between mother and daughter in this drawing is most probably a defense against the wish to separate and become a sexual teenage self.

Figure 4.14 is still another example of preadolescent internalized perceptions of the mother-and-child relationship, drawn by a 12-year-old girl. Here we have good separation, and the girl comes first, an indication of teenage narcissism that is not unusual. However, there is still a good deal of similarity to be observed in stance. The girl seems to be trying to compete, but mother still has broader shoulders and

Figure 4.13. Female, age 11

Figure 4.14. Female, age 12

seems the more powerful of the two. The girl's sexual awareness is indicated once again in the hair emphasis and then denied in the desexualization of both figures. Typical preadolescent body anxiety may be seen in the shading of the shirt.

This next detailed drawing (Figure 4.15) is notable for its impersonality. The 12-year-old boy who drew it called it a "mother-and-child rock." He did not mention that it is also a mother-and-child tree. Or a father-and-child tree, perhaps? Or do both parents partake of some of the qualities of "rockness" or "treeness"?

Consider this drawing a bit more. Note that the qualities of the rock may be considered to be strength, hardness, and coldness—certainly not the human qualities of warmth or relatedness in any sense. In the picture the rocks are close together, though both seem to be in the shelter of the larger tree, which expands beyond the drawing. Perhaps that protective tree reaches out into the rest of the world, offering the child a model for transition to the society beyond the home. The fact that the smaller tree is more heavily drawn perhaps emphasizes it as a self-representation.

The larger, overhanging tree may be seen as both protection and limitation or constriction in the way it hovers over the smaller tree, which is growing up in its shade. This seems to be a nice metaphor for the way a preadolescent boy might perceive his father or other strong external figure. However, the choice of rocks for the mother and child raises questions about the emotional climate in the home.

Teenage Drawings

The task of the adolescent girl is to find her adult female role, which implies both separation from mother and identification with her. However, the boy must make a clear differentiation at adolescence from the mother-figure. Adolescent boys often have more difficulty with the mother-and-child drawing task than do the girls. This is perhaps not surprising, since the girls can identify with the mother as well as the child without sexual-identity conflict. Not so for the boys, who must identify, if at all, with the child, at least at an overt level. During the adolescent struggle that may present great difficulty.

There is a point for many teenage boys in which the mothers that they draw start to look very adolescent, and some boys comment that she looks like his girlfriend. These are all normal indicators of the growth of an adult identity as the boy gains the ability to see himself as a sexual male and a potential father. The child-figure remains the repository of the more infantile parts of the personality in both sexes, and its presentation in the drawing continues to need careful scrutiny at all ages.

Figure 4.15. Male, age 12

Figure 4.16 was drawn by an 18-year-old girl. There is a feminine quality to this drawing, and the mother has a teenage look, appropriate for a girl who now sees more of herself in the mothering role. The more childlike part of her is still seen in the similar child facial and body features. Note that both figures are rather desexualized, and teenage sexual concerns are probably also to be found in the shaded areas, belt emphasis, and heavy feet. These are typical teenage issues. However, the total sense of the picture, both in its placement and constriction to the corner of the paper, seems a bit young for an 18-year-old. Perhaps she is quite protected or insecure, needing to cling to boundaries or to constrict for safety.

Figure 4.17, in contrast, is a drawing by another teenage girl, age 17, with good artistic ability. The profile pose is a difficult one. The mother-figure is completely adult, and the baby is held in her arms. However, there is little warmth in this picture and no eye contact between mother and child. Perhaps this drawing style reflects some coldness in this girl's way of relating to others. Figures are usually

Figure 4.16. Female, age 18

Figure 4.17. Female, age 17

drawn with smiles, and these unsmiling faces may reflect depression, either situational or characterological.

In a completely different style, Figure 4.18 is yet another drawing by a 17-year-old girl. This is not a complete drawing and the artistic skills are minimal, but even so, the warmth and contact is clear as the smiling baby basks in mother's equally smiling gaze. But the lack of the body suggests some avoidance of sexual issues. Perhaps it is easier to focus on the baby after it has already arrived.

Figure 4.19 is by a male adolescent, age 15, who seems to be having a bit of difficulty accepting his growth spurt and the reality of being taller than mother. He places mother on a box to try to even things up. Perhaps he would like to slow down the process of growing up.

Figure 4.20 is by a 16-year-old boy who is clearly losing out in his attempts to assert himself in the mother-and-child relationship. His Superman suit does not work. Note the similarity in the angry, depressed expressions on both figures. However, the mother has a powerful, angry stare, and the boy looks down and away in defeat. Note

Figure 4.18. Female, age 17

Figure 4.19. Male, age 15

Figure 4.20. Male, age 16

the huge emptiness of the mother-figure, the lack of emphasis on her body, and the weakness of the arms in both figures. But also note the emphasis on the legs in the boy, suggesting the beginning of the experience of his own strength and potential for independence. Mother appears to be winning at the moment, but perhaps not for long. If Superman can't fly, perhaps he will run away.

Here again the situation may be pervasive in the boy's relationships, or associated with current reaction to external trauma, but certainly there are issues here for exploration that are often found in teenage circumstances.

Figure 4.21, by an 18-year-old male, presents mother as a teenager, but the body is only outlined. The anxiety about the male-female physical relationship seems to have been displaced onto the boy's shaded shirt and shoes. The figures are constricted and almost lost in the middle of the page.

Some teenage boys resolve the problem of dealing with mothers and children by going into abstractions. Figure 4.22, done by a 19-year-old male, is like a contemporary sculpture. Though very simple, the figures are strong and beautifully integrated, but sculpted together and not separated.

Figure 4.21. Male, age 18

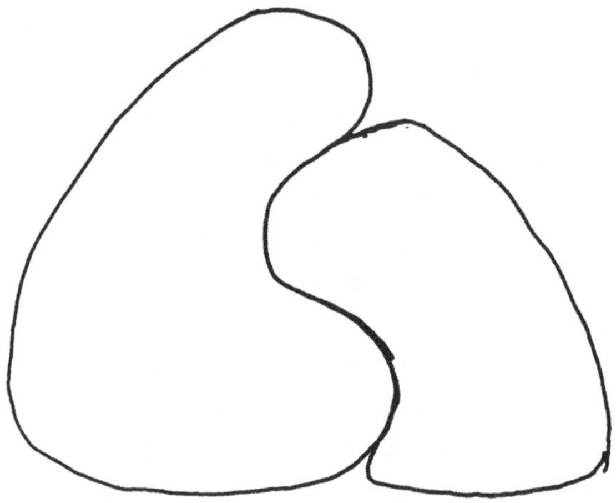

Figure 4.22. Male, age 19

Adult Drawings

Problems with mother-and-child drawings persist into adulthood for many males. Figure 4.23 of a mother-and-child fish was drawn by an adult male, age 38, with a sense of humor, who also had the ability to show the protective caring of the mother for the child and the child's response in a nonhuman presentation. Nevertheless, there seems to be some avoidance of the personal aspects of the relationship through the choice of the nonhuman subject.

Adult women usually enjoy the drawing activity, unless they are uncomfortable with their level of artistic skill.

In Figure 4.24 a young mother, age 34, has attempted the difficult feat of drawing the mother with the child in her lap. Maternal pride and protectiveness are clearly visible in this presentation, but the uncertainty in managing arms, hands, and the child's feet seems less related to the problems inherent in the artistic task than to issues of power and self-assurance.

Figure 4.25 was drawn by a woman, age 42. Note the good drawing skills, which make it easier to see the appropriateness of the portrayed relationship between the mother and son. It would be interesting to have

Figure 4.23. Adult male, age 38

Figure 4.24. Adult female, age 34

Figure 4.25. Adult female, age 42

a drawing from the son, since all mother-and-child drawings reflect a subjective, personal sense of that relationship, which may or may not be shared or seen as objectively accurate by others.

Some women also have trouble with the drawing task and resort to abstract symbolism (Figure 4.26). The 32-year-old woman who drew this has been married for 10 years and has two children. These amorphous shapes, rather like leaves on a plant, have empty spaces for faces and do not seem so much abstract as they do empty, suggesting some difficulty in establishing a firm self-identity on the part of this woman.

Figure 4.27 is a stick-figure evasion of the task by a 35-year-old male, who has nevertheless portrayed the mother with a long neck and the child with none. Standard interpretations since Machover (1949) of the neck in figure drawings consider it evidence of concern with control of body or strong emotional impulses, found here in the mother-figure and completely absent in the presumably more primitive child-figure. It is certainly a typical maternal role to provide the external controls for the more impulse-dominated child. Perhaps those controls remain something of a struggle for this man.

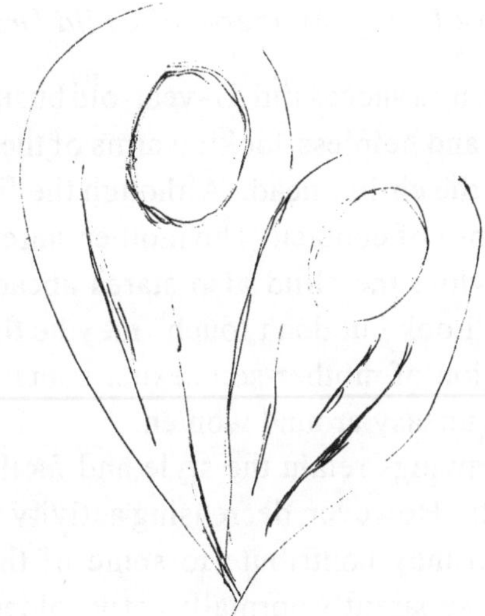

Figure 4.26. Adult female, age 32

Figure 4.27. Adult male, age 35

Figure 4.28, drawn by a successful 57-year-old businessman, shows stiff figures with faint and helpless-looking arms of the mother making tentative contact with the child's head. Although the figures face each other, there is little sense of contact. The mother stares straight ahead with unseeing eyes, while the child also stares ahead, apparently at mother's pubic area. "Look but don't touch" may be the message here in the classic prohibition of mother-son sexual contact. Perhaps this man is still somewhat uneasy around women.

Many later-life drawings retain the style and facility of drawings made by younger adults. However, decreasing activity and opportunity for graphic expression may contribute to some of the more limited drawings presented by apparently normally active older adults. On the other hand, the drawings appear to continue to express current roles and concerns. Figure 4.29, by a busy 71-year-old male, who copes cheerfully with the problems of caring for a chronically ill wife, is rather hesitant. The mother's head looks vaguely male, and the infant in the arms looks very unhappy. The drawing may reflect some inner concerns about his present situation, in which he finds himself very much in the traditional mothering role in relation to his wife. The inner child might be expected to be unhappy about this role reversal.

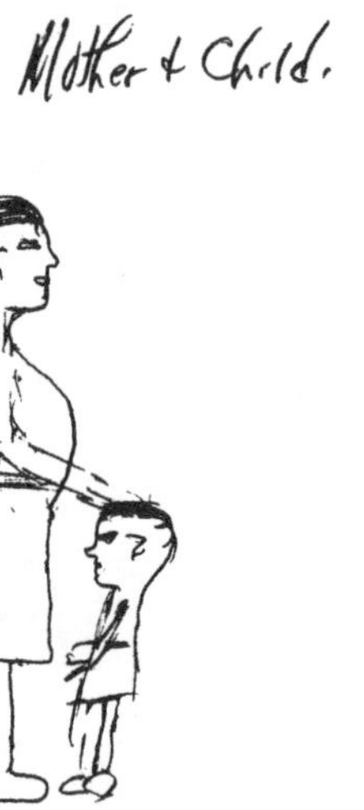

Figure 4.28. Adult male, age 57

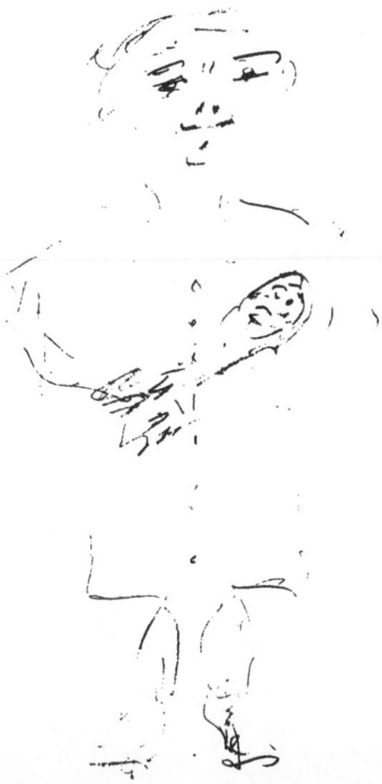

Figure 4.29. Adult male, age 71

SUMMARY AND CONCLUSIONS

In spite of a clear developmental sequence observable in the styles of drawings at various age levels, there is so much individuality in each drawing that it seems important to let each drawing speak for itself to the viewer. The observer is able to try on various possible ideas about a drawing and then check them out for external validation. The drawings often present questions that need to be addressed and expand the possibilities for understanding events and subjective experience that might otherwise be overlooked.

CHAPTER 5

Clinical Issues

GENERAL CONSIDERATIONS

Although it seems possible to describe a general developmental progression in the style of mother-and-child drawings at various ages, the identification of atypical styles, particularly those that may be associated with pathology, must be approached with much more caution. Over the years, the number of research studies on projective person drawings of one kind or another has proliferated. Unfortunately, the findings have been, for the most part, inconclusive and contradictory (see Chapters 1 and 2).

It seems that part of the difficulty with obtaining solid research data lies in the efforts of the investigators to objectify and quantify their material in true experimental style. Most studies attempt, in one fashion or another, to associate specific characteristics of drawings with criterion or categorical variables. For example, it is possible to measure shading as a possible indicator of anxiety and attempt to see if it varies with other measures of anxiety, such as scores on the State-Trait Anxiety Inventory (Spielberger, Gorsach, & Lushene, 1970).

Or, approaching the same issue from another direction, it is possible to obtain drawings from a clinical population of individuals diagnosed as having a generalized anxiety disorder to see if those individuals include more shading in their drawings than a control group. Attempts at this sort of thing have had some slightly positive results, but not nearly enough to warrant reliance on this approach for valid diagnostic results. Even when significant differences are found between groups, the differences may in some instances reflect actual differences in art experiences provided in treatment settings that establish certain approaches to art tasks.

Since the attempts to find specific relationships between drawing characteristics and personality variables continue with unabated enthusiasm, it must be assumed that the amount of intermittent reinforcement obtained from occasional successes keeps the researchers busy at the task. However, the increasing ability to use computer analysis of drawing data may usher in a new era of ability to quantify the data for clearer and more profitable analysis. In any event, statistically significant results derived from normative data may speak only marginally to the needs of the clinician in work with individuals.

The tendency to equate the specifics of drawings with specifics in interpretation is not to be found solely in research studies. The very specific pronouncements about the meaning of the elements in drawings presented by Machover (1949) in her early and very influential material on projective use of person drawings set a pattern of evaluating drawing material that continues today.

However, there are some assumptions inherent in the notion that specific elements in drawings may be associated with certain psychological conditions. Most obviously, it seems necessary to assume a universality of symbolic presentation of personality variables that may be unwarranted. On the other hand, Jungian theory would certainly postulate the existence of collective symbols, resonating throughout a culture, that provide the communication inherent in artistic work of all kinds.

Even if the Jungian thesis is accepted, it remains a long jump to assume that a particular symbol, such as shading representing anxiety, is a predictable way in which anxiety will be presented in drawings. Obviously, there are other ways of presenting anxiety in drawings, a fact that may interfere with certain research designs.

At present, the best validated use of children's drawings in a systematic, diagnostic fashion remains in the area of cognitive development, in the material developed by Harris (1963), based on the earlier work of Goodenough (1926). Harris also presents a cogent and closely reasoned critique of drawings as a measure of personality that retains its value more than 30 years later.

THEORY AND INTERPRETATION

The concepts presented here concerning the projective use of mother-and-child drawings have departed to some extent from the traditional exploration of projective drawings as diagnostic tools and moved to the concept of communication, on a highly individual basis, of aspects of the self and style of relating to others. According to object relations theory, the centrality of the internalized representation of the mother-child relationship is highly influential in the formation of other relationships. The styles of relating developed from the initial experiences of being mothered are also, from that point of view, of crucial significance in the development of personality disorders.

It may be useful, therefore, to explore the overall communication of the mother-and-child drawing, as well as some of the specifics, in order to see how the inner concept of the primary relationship functions for the individual. Atypical presentations communicate something of value concerning the ways in which aspects of that earliest relationship may have gone awry and may continue to be lived out in current relationships.

Drawings, like dreams, may portray wishes and fantasies rather than realities. Wishes may be in the form of defended or idealized presentations, such as the portrayal of a Madonna and Child made by a child in a placement for abandoned children. On the other hand, a quiet, conforming child may produce a drawing that suggests pent-up rage. Such drawings, which contradict the social personality, offer the most value for the clinician. Their content raises questions for further exploration in the therapy hour.

Projection, of course, is not only in the mind of the patient. The drawing as communication from patient to therapist must be read by the therapist, who also has a personal and presumably somewhat different set of internalized notions of the mother-child relationship. The opportunities for bias in interpretation of drawings must always be kept firmly in mind, since the projection on the part of the therapist is an inevitable and inescapable part of the countertransference.

It is well to consider that projections are just that—ways in which aspects of the inner, subjective life are seen in external situations. It seems possible, then, to explore mother-and-child drawings as carrying messages about both (1) experiences of the self and (2) experiences of relationships with significant others.

The following material, then, will approach the interpretation of drawings through asking questions concerning how the material addresses basic self and object relations issues that are central to the needs of the psychotherapeutic relationship.

SYMBOLISM IN DRAWINGS

The symbolism of drawings seems, in many ways, to follow the obvious forms of metaphor that we use daily in casual speech, as well as the larger metaphors that become themes for drama and works of art. Artists use symbols with conscious deliberation and then often find (or others find) that they have introduced other, unconscious material inadvertently. The use of inadvertent symbolism in mother-and-child drawings establishes the form that projection takes, and we must interpret the content of the drawings through understanding the symbolism. That symbolism takes on special focus in mother-and-child drawings through their emphasis on the relationship and the forms of connectedness, or lack of connectedness, between the figures.

Socially, the initial indication of willingness to make contact may be seen in the smile, a very basic and prosaic symbol for human interaction. The smile may also be used as a defense to ward off anticipated attack or to belie inner feelings of hostility. So omnipresent are the smiling faces in advertising on TV, billboards, and in print media that we have all been conditioned to an automatic smiling greeting in new encounters. It is not surprising, then, that almost all human figure drawings are done with smiling faces, and the exceptions are rare enough to warrant careful attention. Smiling, eye contact, physical contact, and reaching out are all ways of portraying positive aspects of relationships. Mother-and-child drawings with this content carry a positive communication.

On the other hand, reaching out may also be done in ways that are less benign. Moving toward may also be a form of moving against. We talk about the fellow who "claws his way to the top," using the metaphor of the primitive and dangerous animal to describe ruthless behavior. Mother-and-child drawings may evoke aggressive and competitive content and control issues, as well as nurturance and support. Sometimes mother has long, clawlike fingers. Perhaps the child has them instead. Or perhaps both figures have long, hostile fingernails. If both figures have aggressive-looking hands, then the overt expression or at least acknowledgment of hostility issues is more likely. If only one figure has them, then the issue is more probably conflicted, and the nature of the projection requires further consideration.

Wide-open, screaming mouths also suggest anger, and perhaps also pain. Again, which of the duo seems to be doing the screaming? The apparent duality reflects inner conflict, even if that conflict arises from actual hostile encounters in the daily life of the individual.

Therefore, it is possible that the portrayal of an attacking mother may have an accurate basis in an external situation, but it is the internal representation of an attacking mother that may cause difficulty in, say, authority relationships at work. The internalized critical mother may continue to cause trouble in later relationships, long after she is only a marginal part of an individual's adult life or even after her death.

Relationships may be viewed as either seeking or avoiding closeness. The move toward closeness may be either positive and loving or hostile and destructive. The need for distance is also valid. Actual relationships partake of all of those forms of contact, or lack of contact, in some amalgam of feelings. Mother-and-child drawings seem to have something to say about a pervasive set of attitudes toward these issues.

CLINICAL EXAMPLES

Developmental Delays

The residue of early symbiotic ties that still operate in current adult dependency conflicts seems to appear most commonly in the portrayal of mother and child as two children, in child proportions, either alike or very similar. The developmental sequence in mother-and-child drawings presented in Chapter 4 shows that style to be typical of young children. It is also typical of the mentally retarded, whose drawings parallel their mental age rather than their chronological age (see Harris, 1963).

Figure 5.1, for example, is the drawing of a retarded 18-year-old girl (IQ in the low 50s), who is cheerful, well cared for, and apparently content. It is very comparable in style to the drawings of the young children presented in the developmental section and certainly has little in common with the teen drawings. It suggests that this young woman's self-experience is that of a young child and that her relationships are still seen in terms of her dependencies on others. Her limitations place realistic constraints on her ability to develop a sense of herself as a self-reliant and independent adult.

However, it seems important to note here that this drawing reflects not just the cognitive limitations associated with mental retardation but also a parallel lack of development in the personality and sense of relating to others that is also part of the pattern of slow and partial development of the self in the retarded.

Figure 5.1. Female, age 18

Figure 5.2 is another drawing, done by a younger retarded child, which presents the same issues as those in the previous teen drawing but at an earlier developmental level. The 9-year-old who drew this picture has not yet developed a drawing style that includes a body on his figures, a drawing approach more typical of children ages 3 to 5, and which certainly suggests delays in establishing a sense of body identity. The figures are almost identical, except for the feet, where clear differentiation is made. These figures get around on those firmly drawn legs and feet, and the facial features appear to offer contact. But those appendages that may be arms instead of ears do not offer much in the way of establishing control or competence, probably a realistic social perception of the self. This child is still under the protection of the parenting involved in the earlier stages of development, where demands for social maturation can be kept suitably limited, both at home and in school.

Figure 5.3 is a drawing by a 15-year-old girl, mildly retarded (IQ in the 60s) but with more behavioral disturbance. Note the increased differentiation between the figures in comparison with the previous drawing, but also note the open mouth with the aggressive-looking teeth in the mother-figure. This girl is considered "mouthy"; she has a great deal of difficulty accepting criticism and denies her verbal aggression.

Figure 5.2. Male, age 9

Figure 5.3. Female, age 15

The child-figure here is smiling sweetly and the mother is the "mouthy" one. The figures carry a split self-projection—the good child and the verbally aggressive and powerful mother.

Although this girl has cognitive limitations, her issues seem less developmental than behavioral, and it is important here to see that the drawing, which may be characterized as in line with her mental age, offers a number of other issues for conjecture. Because this girl carries a primary diagnosis of mental retardation (which may be inappropriate, given her oppositional behavior and possible lack of cooperation in testing), there is a temptation to assume that her social difficulties arise from her inability to understand at a cognitive level the requirements of social interaction.

This drawing suggests exploration of issues concerning how aggressive feelings are managed in the family. Who is allowed to express anger? Under what circumstances? Where else might denial be observed? Perhaps the mother is indeed verbally or otherwise aggressive, but that one-to-one assumption cannot be made from the drawing. What are the family expectations for this girl? How do they handle her limitations?

After considering this relatively more mature drawing, let us now return to a primitive one, this time a drawing done by a 21-year-old young man with cerebral palsy and moderate mental retardation (Figure 5.4). The first figure (the left one), he said, was himself; the scribbling on top of the head was hair, and the decoration around the face was a beard. The second figure was mother, on her knees in church. He called attention to the extra hair he had given her. (Preoccupation with hair during early teens is extremely common, since during that time the development of body hair associated with sexual characteristics is a source of both pride and anxiety. The hair issue may be seen in teenagers and their constant concern with hairstyles, carrying hairbrushes, etc.) In this young adult male the focus on this issue suggests his ongoing struggle to accept himself, and have others accept him, as fully sexual, a chronic and very difficult issue for the disabled.

The style of drawing, like that of the 9-year-old presented earlier, is without a body form. In that child, however, we could be comfortable that the drawing was compatible with his mental age. This young man, with cerebral palsy severe enough to require wheelchair confinement, has the added burden of the actual distortion of his physical body experience to provide limitations in the growth of a psychological body image. Although he is certainly appropriately classified as mentally retarded on the basis of the usual criteria not relevant here, he is certainly not so limited as the drawing would suggest.

Figure 5.4. Male, age 21

But it is extremely important for the understanding of drawings to notice that the limited development of a body image for this young man appears to be associated with the undeveloped drawing of the body figures, and that the style of the drawing is quite in line with the drawings routinely provided by very young children. There are, of course, important implications for working with this young man, who must deal with social and sexual concerns with little coherent sense of body self in which to anchor his understandings.

The possibility of pseudoretardation always lurks in the background in assessments of mental retardation. In that regard the use of drawings can be most helpful as supportive evidence. Since drawings typically follow developmental age rather than chronological age, drawings by the mentally retarded may be expected to be appropriate for the mental age. If not, then other issues should be explored.

For example, let us look at Figure 5.5, drawn by a 7-year-old girl. This 7-year-old is a very quiet, withdrawn child in a program for developmentally delayed children. Her current provisional diagnosis is mild mental retardation. But this drawing has little in common, except

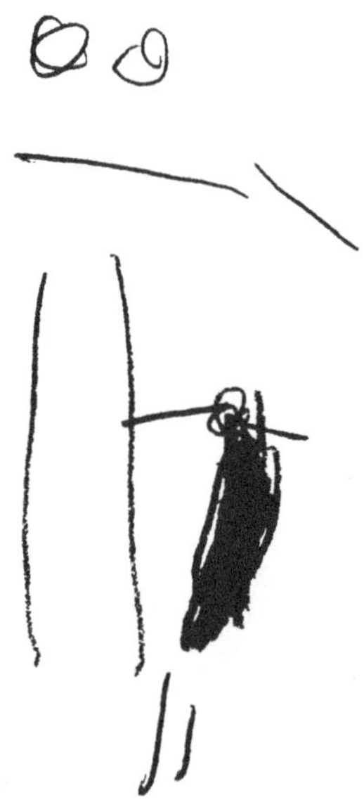

Figure 5.5. Female, age 7

for its sparseness of detail, with the drawings obtained from other mentally retarded children.

There is differentiation here; the blackened child-figure (suggesting serious depression and an internalized "bad" self) clings to the amorphous mother. There is contact between the two figures, but the subjective "feel" of the picture does not communicate that contact as warmth in a relationship.

These figures suggest an entirely different set of internal perceptions of self and other from those obtained in the previous drawings of the developmentally delayed. A careful observation of the circumstances of this child's life should be undertaken. Possibilities of abuse and/or neglect, or a seriously deprived background, may be found. On the other hand, there may be indications of a schizophrenic process. The child's placement in a program for the developmentally delayed was a trial placement for evaluation purposes.

Sometimes a need for protection or for boundaries can be symbolized by placing the figures in a house. The following two drawings choose that solution, the first (Figure 5.6) drawn by a developmentally

Figure 5.6. Male, age 9

disabled boy, age 9, and the second (Figure 5.7) by an 8-year-old boy with attention deficit disorder (ADD).

Note the differences in the styles of drawing, even though both use the protective house. The developmentally disabled boy is trying to be well organized, within the limits of his ability. The lines are carefully completed and appear to be done with deliberation. Perhaps the need for safety is important here.

In contrast, the boy with ADD seems to have hurtled through the drawing process, impatient to finish the task, with hasty, scribbled line quality that probably reflects his general approach to tasks. The need for controls and boundaries appears to be more prominent here. In both cases the figures are proportionately large and fill the houses, a grandiose perspective that may be positive for these boys at present.

The placement of the two pictures is different. Top-of-page placement of Figure 5.6 suggests a more positive outlook than Figure 5.7, which is placed at the base of the page. The metaphor of feeling "down" is a common one to signify a period of depression, and bottom placement (base of page) of drawings is usually construed as reflecting

Figure 5.7. Male, age 8

depressive moods or need for "grounding." Attention-deficit children are often in trouble for their behavior, and there are notions that some hyperactivity may be a form of manic defense against depression.

Atypical development of various kinds typically requires adaptations in relations with others and continuing emotional dependency needs, even if productive social roles have been established. For example, Figure 5.8 is the drawing of a 17-year-old boy with a long history of severe learning disabilities. His family has been very supportive. He is rather quiet but socially well accepted, and he has already established and is moving toward good vocational objectives.

But this drawing shows a clinging little boy hanging on to a protective and aggressive mother. Both bodies are heavily shaded, suggesting pervasive anxiety and depression. The mother appears to be allowed to be verbally aggressive, but the small boy stares at us with a placating smile. Perhaps the observable social conformity in this boy's behavior is at odds with a desire to be more aggressive. Fear of self-assertion and anxiety about the possible destructive power of aggressive feelings are often found in individuals with atypical development; this makes them more than usually dependent on powerful and protective adults.

Figure 5.8. Male, age 17

Figure 5.9 displays another manifestation of a different issue but the same general problem in establishing an adult identity. The 18-year-old man who drew this picture is deaf. He has moved along well in academic work and has appropriate, high-level vocational goals. He is bright and responsible but socially isolated, as is often the case with the deaf. The most obvious characteristic of this drawing is the absence of the bodies. (Mother-and-child drawings are accepted as presented, without insistence that the "whole person" be drawn. However, a second drawing request for whole persons would have been useful.)

Almost equally obvious is the unusual and compulsive attention to detail in the faces, which seems very appropriate in a young man who must rely constantly on his visual ability to read the nuances of facial expression. His social communication rests in his lip-reading ability.

Since his ability to express himself verbally is quite limited, he must invite acceptance from others with a smile, but that smile over prominent, clenched teeth may be quite defensive. Problems with bodies, aggressive feelings, and sexuality seem not to be consciously considered as yet. Note the individuality and vividness of the drawings, which are good portraits of himself and his mother.

Figure 5.9. Male, age 18

Symbiosis

Symbiotic issues are related to problems of separation and formation of an individual self. When mother and child are drawn as alike, there is the possibility that there is an interior perception of the self and mother as still merged in some fashion.

Figures 5.10 and 5.11 are two drawings by a little boy, age 5. His person drawing (Figure 5.10) is almost completely blacked out, which seems to be more depressive than anxious because of its intensity and bottom-of-the-page placement. The "social" smile is not very convincing. Instead, it seems as if the boy is trying to destroy the figure with heavy and overworked black penciling.

Note that in the child's mother-and-child drawing (Figure 5.11) the shading has disappeared. Now there are two almost identical figures with hands tightly linked. The child-figure seems happy now in his symbiotic reunion with the mother.

This boy has 3-year-old triplet sisters, born when he was age 2, during the period of development considered the most important in the separation-individuation process (Mahler, Pine, & Bergman, 1975).

Figure 5.10. Male, age 5

Figure 5.11. Male, age 5

This child did indeed lose his place with mother when his sisters were born, out of the sheer necessity, since the mother had to invest most of her time in the girls. At present, he constantly seeks attention from his schoolteacher, withdraws and sulks when he is ignored, and is aggressive toward other children. On a one-to-one basis, he is cooperative and cheerful. There is a tendency to consider him as spoiled and demanding.

Demanding he certainly is, but not spoiled. Therapy needs to be designed to provide the missing attention he did not receive at age-appropriate times so that he can move ahead developmentally.

The issue of how much and what kind of attention he receives in the home at present needs to be explored. Habits of focusing on the triplets may have, by now, pushed this boy into the background routinely.

Figure 5.12 is a similar drawing from a 6-year-old girl who is being considered for retention in the first grade. Although she has no such dramatic history of disruptive events in her life as those portrayed in the previous situation, she exhibits some of the same behaviors, along with academic retardation. What is the family style of giving—or not giving—to this child?

Unfortunately, this condition is not rare. There are many demanding children who let us know how badly they need attention. Because they are so needy, they try to establish a symbiosis with the teacher, who finds their constant insatiable demands untenable. Not surprisingly, these children receive additional rejection as a result.

Figure 5.12. Female, age 6

When the same style of drawing appears in the work of adults, the results are even more striking. Note here the work of adult women: Figure 5.13 is similar to drawings done by children approximately 8 years of age, which were featured in the developmental section (see Figures 4.6 and 4.7); however, Figure 5.13 was drawn by a 44-year-old woman. The handless figures in this drawing appear even more helpless than the figures in the children's drawings. Figure 5.14, drawn by a 57-year-old woman, shows similar handless figures, but with one set of hands tightly interlocked; this drawing is extremely primitive in execution, in a style reflective of symbiotic similarity. The 44-year-old woman was a volunteer from a church group, from which a half dozen other drawings were unremarkable and adult in style. The 57-year-old was a member of a weight control group. Both appeared quite dependent and eager to please.

It is difficult to tell, without clinical assessment, what the circumstances of these women's lives may be. However, there may be many adults, and particularly older women, who live very conformist-style lives and who give no evidence of internal loneliness and distress in the course of their daily activities. Society recognizes and gives approval to a good deal of dependency needs in women, and they may remain in family situations that support their dependency. However, some also regress as a result of changing roles and loss of emotional support systems. It would be interesting to know if such were the case in these situations.

Figure 5.13. Female, age 44

Figure 5.14. Female, age 57

The young man who created Figure 5.15 drew his faint figures with large, aggressively smiling mouths. He was a 13-year-old who had worn out three residential private school placements in 16 months. He was extraordinarily demanding and self-centered. He was actively rejected by his peers, and barely tolerated by adults. However, his mother doted on him, supported his excesses and his misbehavior, and generally made his adaptation more and more difficult. It seemed she had created a child that only a mother could love. (Perhaps she needed a child who would have no other relationships. Possibly her own symbiotic needs are expressed in the boy's behavior and their style of relating.)

The boy's basic uncertainty was apparent only in these figures, which show the apparently confident façade only in the large mouths of the figures. Fragility is indicated in the line quality and the childlike buttons (by most criteria, evidence of dependency) on the figures, which are indeed much alike.

But the striking quality of this drawing is the way in which the drawing was done. He drew the boy first, though it is on the right side of the drawing. He drew the upper part of the body, omitting the facial features, and then went down the connecting arm, drew the interlocked hands, and then went up the arm of the mother-figure and completed her

Figure 5.15. Male, age 13

upper torso in the same style as the other figure. He then completed the figures, alternating his attention between the two. The facial features were completed last.

The boy's drawing behavior suggests unusual merger qualities in the relationship between mother and child. It would be interesting to explore this boy's expectations from others, and what he feels others expect from him. How do his dependency needs associated with his mother affect his relationships with peers? With adults? What about his attempts to break away, if he dares?

Severe Emotional Disturbance

Individuals who have lost touch with reality express their own distorted logics and preoccupations in their drawings. Schizophrenic art has long been a source of study, and in the freedom to express without limits, some remarkable productions have been observed. The mother-and-child task, however, is a specific and limited one and thus offers structure that tends to limit the spillover of fantasy material into the drawing content. Nevertheless, the irrational is more freely presented in the work of persons categorized as emotionally disturbed, and certain oddities and idiosyncracies occur that are highly individual.

Although most drawings could be associated with a number of diagnostic categories, or perhaps none, once in a while a drawing can, in itself, be described as a "crazy" or psychotic drawing. Figure 5.16, with its nude figures and explicit presentation of genitalia, is clearly aberrant, even without the knowledge that it was done by a 19-year-old male diagnosed as paranoid schizophrenic in a juvenile detention facility psychiatric service. It is interesting to note that the two figures, which have been endowed with heavily emphasized genitals, seem oddly asexual. Perhaps this individual has very little capacity to relate to others, and it shows.

It is also interesting to note that there is no real "child" figure here. Perhaps the inner child is undeveloped or destroyed and relates only to aggressive sexuality in any possible contact with others. Rape or other kinds of assaults on persons may be associated with this type of drawing, and the possibility of early molestation in his background is worth exploring.

But all paranoid schizophrenics do not produce such dramatically disturbed drawings. Figure 5.17 was drawn by a 15-year-old male delinquent, carrying the same diagnosis in the same facility. This young

Figure 5.16. Male, age 19

Figure 5.17. Male, age 15

man is alternately homicidal and suicidal. Note the tiny, floating child, who looks like a girl and tends to duplicate the mother-figure in many ways. Perhaps there are borderline and symbiotic issues here, with periodic decompensation into psychosis. The oddly wide neck is often considered to offer too little separation between head and body, or, symbolically, between primitive feelings (body) and ego control (head). Are those raised arms in both figures asking for help?

A small, floating child is also found in even more dramatic fashion in Figure 5.18, which shows a well-detailed head of a young woman and a very tiny, floating, twisting infant beside her. A very unusual treatment indeed, especially considering the artistic skill of the portrayals. What does it say about the helpless inner child of this 18-year-old schizophrenic male delinquent?

Figure 5.19 is a drawing showing a curiously shaped neck on the child only, an adult daughter who is entirely separated from the mother as they appear on different levels. Mother comes first and seems to have more control over herself, if we interpret the normal neck as being symbolic of this situation. Note the tiny, ineffectual arms on the daughter. This drawing was produced by an 18-year-old girl with a

Figure 5.18. Male, age 18

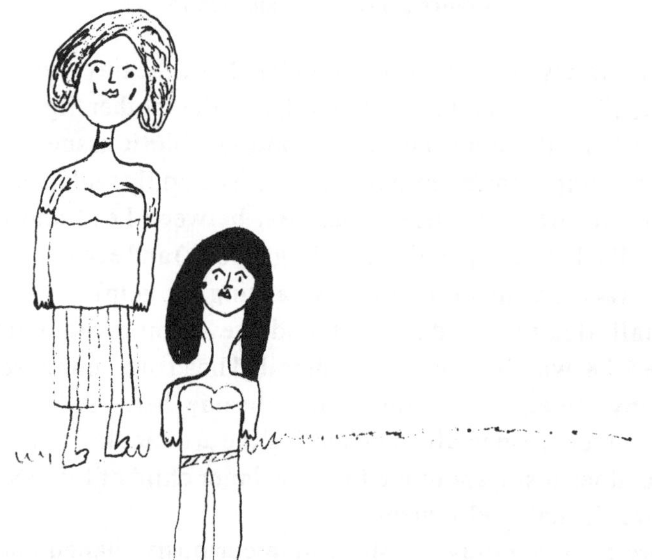

Figure 5.19. Female, age 18

diagnosis of schizophrenia, undifferentiated. Does this young woman identify most closely at an unconscious level with the more damaged child-figure? Does she see the possibility of becoming more like her notion of the adult mother? The mother-figure is more faint. Would she prefer not to grow up and remain a more uninhibited child?

Figures 5.20, 5.21, and 5.22 were produced by a schizophrenic young man, age 18, who had been in and out of mental hospitals since he was a young child. He created and appears to live the most meaningful part of his life in a sort of science fiction fantasy world where all the inhabitants are body builders and engage in marvelous displays of muscle. He did these drawings in one session, beginning with the Draw-a-Person. Figure 5.20, labeled John Hinkley, was a theme drawing with him. He enjoyed drawing this figure and would do so often, even without invitation. He was asked to do the mother-and-child drawing next, and responded immediately with the tiny figures in Figure 5.21. Figure 5.21 is in such contrast to Figure 5.20 that I wondered if something had occurred other than the drawing task to produce such a change in drawing style. He was then asked to do a House-Tree-Person in a composite picture, and the third drawing (Figure 5.22) was the result. The return to the D-A-P drawing style was immediate, although the arms are now much more powerful.

Figure 5.20. Male, age 18

Figure 5.21. Male, age 18

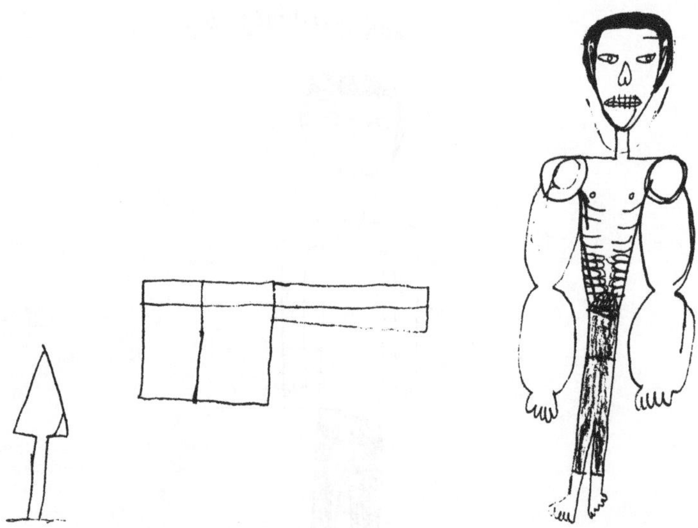

Figure 5.22. Male, age 18

This boy's behavior suggests that the mother-and-child drawing may, now and then, tap something different from the usual projective material. It is impossible to know what occasioned that change in drawing style. When asked, the boy shrugged indifferently and went on with his own concerns. However, it just seems possible that the return to the symbiotic relationship with mother brings him back to reality, but at the cost of reducing him to insignificance and shattering his grandiose fantasies. This phenomenon recalls the drawings in Figures 5.10 and 5.11, where the figures in the mother-and-child drawing appear to improve in quality over the depressive person-drawing.

Minnesota Multiphasic Personality Inventory Comparisons

The comparison of drawings with more objective measures is always useful. Here are MMPI profiles, along with mother-and-child drawings, from three late-teenage juvenile delinquents identified as severely emotionally disturbed. The MMPI profiles differ and, of course, so do the drawings.

The first MMPI profile (Figure 5.23A) is that of a young adult male in a psychiatric facility, carrying a diagnosis of paranoid schizophrenia. His drawing (Figure 5.23B) is quite peculiar, with relatively normal-appearing heads on top of strange, boxlike bodies. The mother-figure is empty, and the child-figure is filled in with jagged lines, which seems to say something about the conflicts in the inner life of this individual. Both figures have talon claws for hands, but the mother has shaded arms, perhaps to represent some social anxiety about aggression, either experienced or projected or both. Note that the anxiety is seen in the more mature part of the personality, represented by the mother-figure, while the child-figure retains more of the aggression.

The second MMPI profile (Figure 5.24A) reflects a different type of disturbance in which depression is a major feature. In the drawing (Figure 5.24B), note the empty figures, with hands held in contact but apparently with so little to give. Empty, poorly defined figures seem to be found often with depression and identity disorders.

The third profile (Figure 5.25A) appears much less disturbed and more like a standard acting-out, relatively normal profile, with defensiveness reflected in the high K scale. The drawing (Figure 5.25B) shows extremely tiny figures along the bottom of the page, probably reflecting psychological size and feelings of insignificance defended against by aggressive behavior.

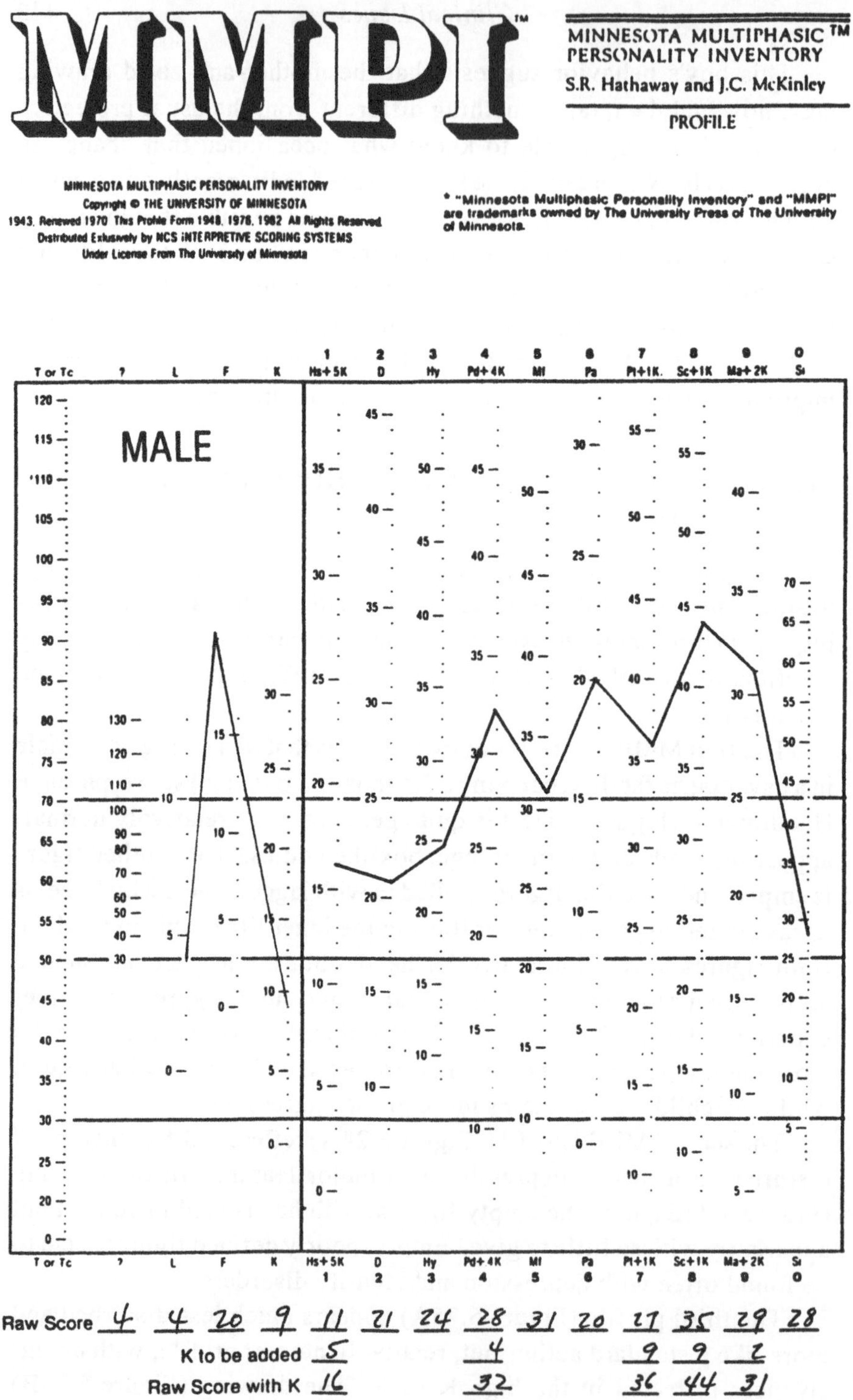

Figure 5.23A. Male, late teen

Figure 5.23B. Male, late teen

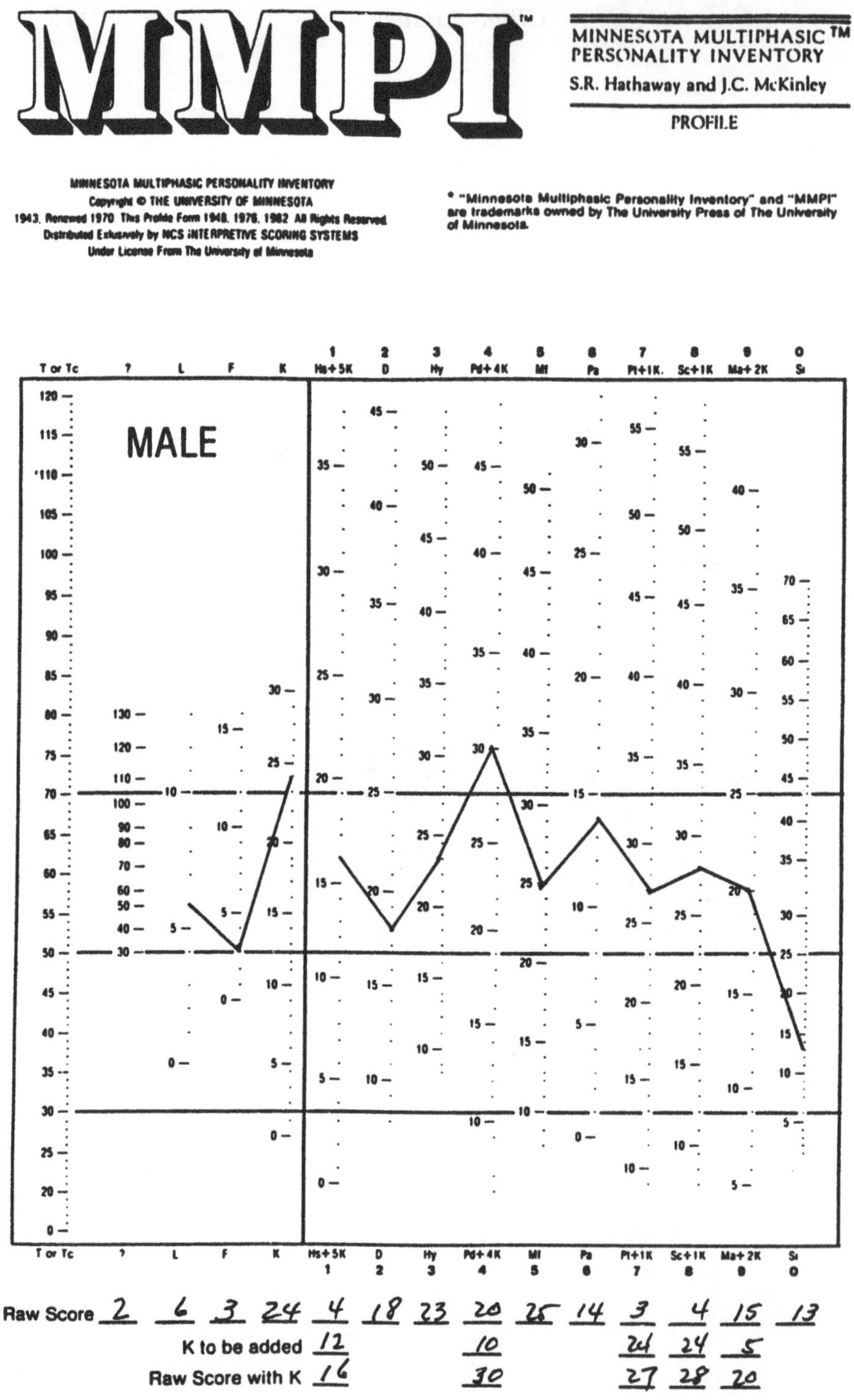

Figure 5.25A. Male, late teen

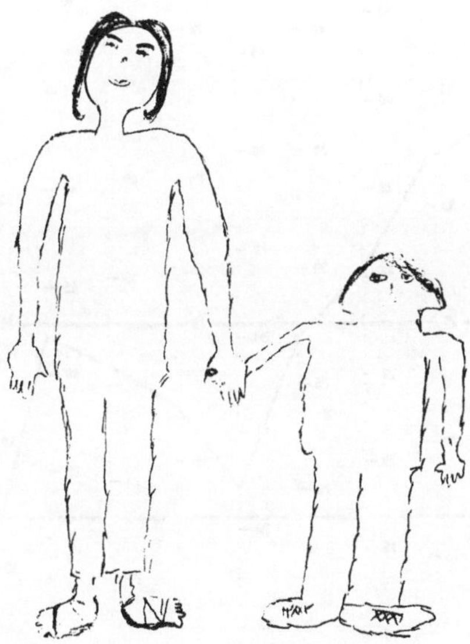

Figure 5.24B. Male, late teen

MMPI™

MINNESOTA MULTIPHASIC™ PERSONALITY INVENTORY

S.R. Hathaway and J.C. McKinley

PROFILE

MMPI Code

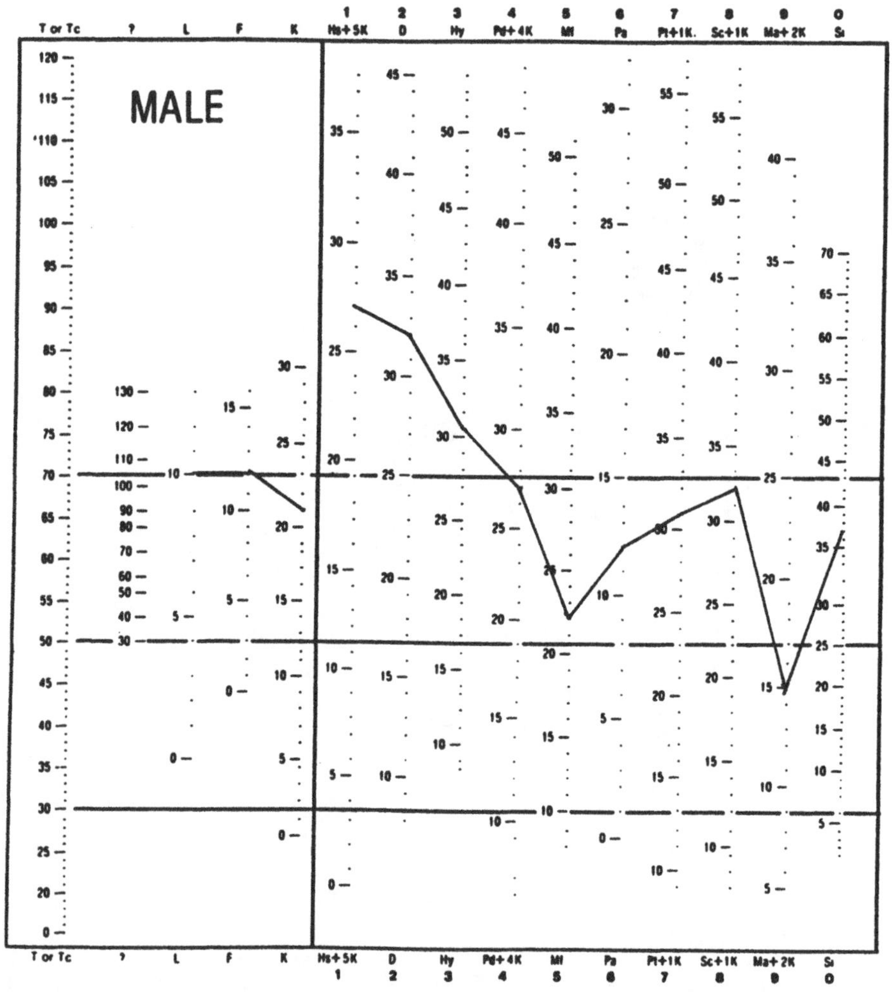

	?	L	F	K	Hs+5K	D	Hy	Pd+4K	Mf	Pa	Pt+1K	Sc+1K	Ma+2K	Si
Raw Score	0	10	12	21	16	32	31	19	22	12	10	11	11	37
K to be added					11			8			21	21	4	
Raw Score with K					27			27			31	32	15	

Figure 5.40A. Male, teen

Figure 5.25B. Male, late teen

Borderline Issues

The comments concerning symbiosis are, of course, relevant to the ways in which individuals with borderline issues present those issues in drawings. However, here I present some examples of other ways in which those conflicts may be represented. Typically, individuals with borderline problems are involved in very intense but conflicted personal relationships, as they try both to cling to and break away from symbiotic relationships. Drawings may reflect the symbiosis directly, or more specific attention may be paid to the conflicts.

Figure 5.26, for example, is a cartooned figure done by a hospitalized 14-year-old male with a diagnosis of conduct disorder and borderline personality organization. Mother holds on to him, but rejects him at the same time, and his behavior in the drawing invites repetition of that maternal response. The drawing graphically represents the quandary of this boy. The use of cartoon figures is common in teenage boys, who find it possible to present important issues in that fashion while denying that they have serious significance. The cartoons also seem to represent the protective mask behind which they can hide while dealing with their circumstances.

Figure 5.26. Male, age 14

Figures 5.27 and 5.28 are two drawings from an 8-year-old girl, which show similar conflicts. The mother carries a borderline diagnosis, and the child displays many borderline traits. This 8-year-old was reluctant to do the first drawing (Figure 5.27) and started with a giant house in the middle of the page (probably anger at the therapist merging into the internalized image of a dominating mother-figure), and two trees that appear to set limits for the expansiveness of the house. The house is poorly defined, with high, inaccessible windows as its major embellishment. The heavily shaded walkway turns away from the figures after promising access. The child drew the mother-figure without arms, which were added last after much argument with herself. She drew mother cross-eyed (so that she couldn't see?—remember the eye/window emphasis on the house) and added buttons to her lips to "shut her up," she said with glee. There also seems to be another mother-and-child relationship in the animals on the other side of the page. The bunny watches while the tiny mouse scurries to its hole. There is a great deal of content in this drawing, but for present purposes it is important primarily to point out the heavy dependency on mother and the anger and conflict engendered within that relationship.

Figure 5.27. Female, age 8

The use of the House-Tree-Person material by Buck (1948, 1966) suggests that each drawing, done on separate sheets of paper, reflects the self. In young children, however, it seems often most appropriate to see the house as mother and the tree as father. Asking the child to draw a house, a tree, and a person and make them all into a picture provides a sense of the relationships within the Oedipal triad. This style of H-T-P drawings is not unusual; in fact, though not described as an alternative, there are illustrations using this format in Oster and Gould (1987, pp. 45 & 46). In this case, the instructions were to draw a mother and child, and the extraneous but very useful material was embellishment provided by the child.

The same child drew another mother and child several months later, near Thanksgiving. In Figure 5.28 we have a tiny baby turkey following along behind a mother turkey (with closed or sightless eyes this time) as they move through a storm. Note that the relationship implies that the child must take care of its own needs as best it can and does so through dependency on mother, who appears to go her own way without attention to the child.

Figure 5.28. Female, age 8

The next drawings are by mothers of 7-year-olds. The first drawing (Figure 5.29) shows a rather faint and resentful-looking mother raising a faint but aggressive hand over a vividly presented and aggressive little boy. But the little boy has rather feminine features and presumably also represents the inner feelings of aggression that she must project onto the child. This young mother feels that she cannot manage her child. Perhaps her own denied needs to assert herself and vicarious enjoyment of her son's behavior are being expressed in her drawing. Dependency issues here certainly need exploration.

The second drawing (Figure 5.30) is very different in kind. Here the dependency is very overt, as the mother holds the child in front of her, retained within her own body image in an odd sort of midline emphasis that could be very narcissistic. Note the transparency of the mother's lower body, with the incorporated child within.

Figure 5.29. Female, age 27

Figure 5.30. Female, age 38

Splitting

The concept of splitting internal representations of objects into good and bad can also be seen in drawings. In mother-and-child drawings the child is seldom seen as good with an apparently bad mother, although the child may be seen as bad with a relatively good mother. ("Good" may be defined here as appropriately drawn, with pleasant facial expression, and "bad" as angry appearing and/or distorted.) The need to see the self as bad in order to protect the image of the good mother seems to be a common one that results in low self-esteem and depression.

Figures 5.31, 5.32, and 5.33 are three drawings, done by teenage boys, which are different in style, but they have a single theme. The babies are all held in arms, and they are all scribbled out with heavy pencil markings. The mothers are unshaded. These drawings suggest that the inner self, the child within, is seen as bad or perhaps as dead. The mother-figures are poor in quality, but the heavy shading appears only on the child. These drawings were chosen from drawings by groups of high school students without apparent pathology.

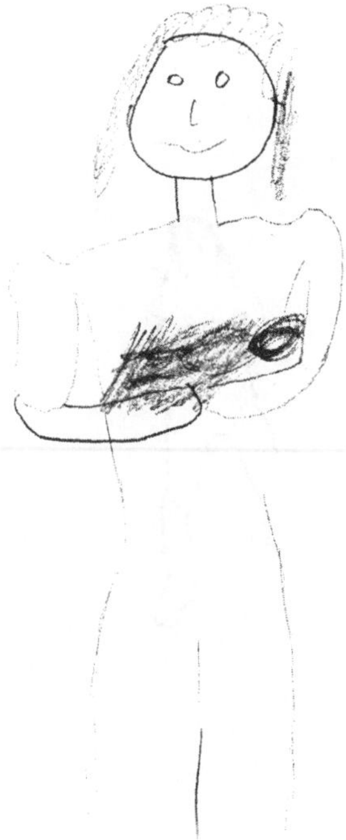

Figure 5.31. Male, teen

Figure 5.32. Male, teen

Figure 5.33. Male, teen

Figure 5.34 represents another form of splitting, in which mother and child have reciprocal omissions in drawing detail. This drawing was also done by a teenage boy. In this drawing, the body of the mother is almost empty, but the body of the child is well detailed. In contrast, the child has no mouth, but the mother has an emphasized mouth. This boy may be having trouble attributing feelings, and probably sexuality, to mother. It may be safer not talk about those feelings and also to let mother do the talking. Perhaps she does anyway. Or perhaps the split is more complete, and the boy must not permit himself to identify at the feeling level with mother because of his own need to establish himself as heterosexual at his teen level of development and deny possible homosexual feelings. In any case, the internal conflict represented by this drawing appears extensive but typical of teenage developmental concerns.

Figure 5.34. Male, teen

Organicity

Disturbance of personality resulting from organicity is often reflected in drawings, usually in overall weakness in form and distortions in detail.

Figure 5.35, for example, is a drawing obtained from an 18-year-old male with a diagnosis of organic mental disorder, substance induced. There is a history of multiple substance abuse over a period of years. Note the off-balance appearance of the figures as well as the primitive quality of the productions.

The possibility of organic deterioration also may be reflected in the drawings of the elderly, even when no overt evidence of reduced capacity is observed. Figure 5.36 was drawn by a 68-year-old male, apparently normally active and alert. It raises some questions about his neurological integrity, since the apparent perceptual distortion here cannot be accounted for by any known medical or emotional problems. Careful observation and complete assessment seems warranted.

Figure 5.35. Male, age 18

Figure 5.36. Male, age 68

Figure 5.37 was drawn by a woman, age 76, with a diagnosis of Alzheimer's syndrome. She wrote the words "Mother & Child Picture," probably to help her remember the task while she worked on it. Even so, she completed only the first shape. The second one, peeking over the edge of the paper, was added (in contradiction to basic instructions) at the urging of a nursing assistant who was supervising the task. The deterioration represented by this drawing is clear without further comment.

Ego Defenses

Defensive organizations of behaviors are often reflected in drawings also. For example, compulsivity in drawing style may be easily observed in excessive attention to detail.

The 16-year-old girl who drew Figure 5.38 seemed to go on forever, as she carefully drew each ringlet of hair and each eyelash on each figure. Clothing details were attended to in the same way, although much of that detail is not apparent in the reproductions. However, it is important to note the underlying insecurity that calls forth the compulsivity, since the figures are incomplete, with legs and feet not drawn. The drawings are positioned so that the bottom of the page intervenes.

Figure 5.37. Female, age 76

Figure 5.38. Female, age 16

Figure 5.39 is a most remarkable one, obtained from a 12-year-old boy whose father was a military officer charged with child abuse. This artistically very competent picture presents a mother-and-child dragon, but another figure has been added. The dragon-slayer, in a full suit of armor and brandishing a phallic sword, is ready to do battle. The heavy pencil emphasis in the picture is on the dragon-slayer, in spite of the size and ferocity of the mother dragon. Note also the similarity between mother and baby dragon.

This picture seems to be a rather dramatic example of the beginnings of identification with the aggressor (see Sandler with Freud, 1985), in which the abused child learns to identify with the abusing father and becomes, in turn, an abuser to his own children. Perhaps therapy for the child, as well as the father, will break this family pattern.

Here is another MMPI profile (Figure 5.40A) from the disturbed delinquent population, reflecting strong tendencies toward somatization of problems. It is interesting to note that the mother-and-child drawing shows a helpless child stretched out on a table or bed, while a huge teen mother-figure stares out at us and ignores him.

The general content of Figure 5.41 is surprisingly similar to the previous drawing, though it was done by a 12-year-old girl who was a

Figure 5.39. Male, age 12

MMPI™

MINNESOTA MULTIPHASIC ™
PERSONALITY INVENTORY

S.R. Hathaway and J.C. McKinley

PROFILE

MMPI Code

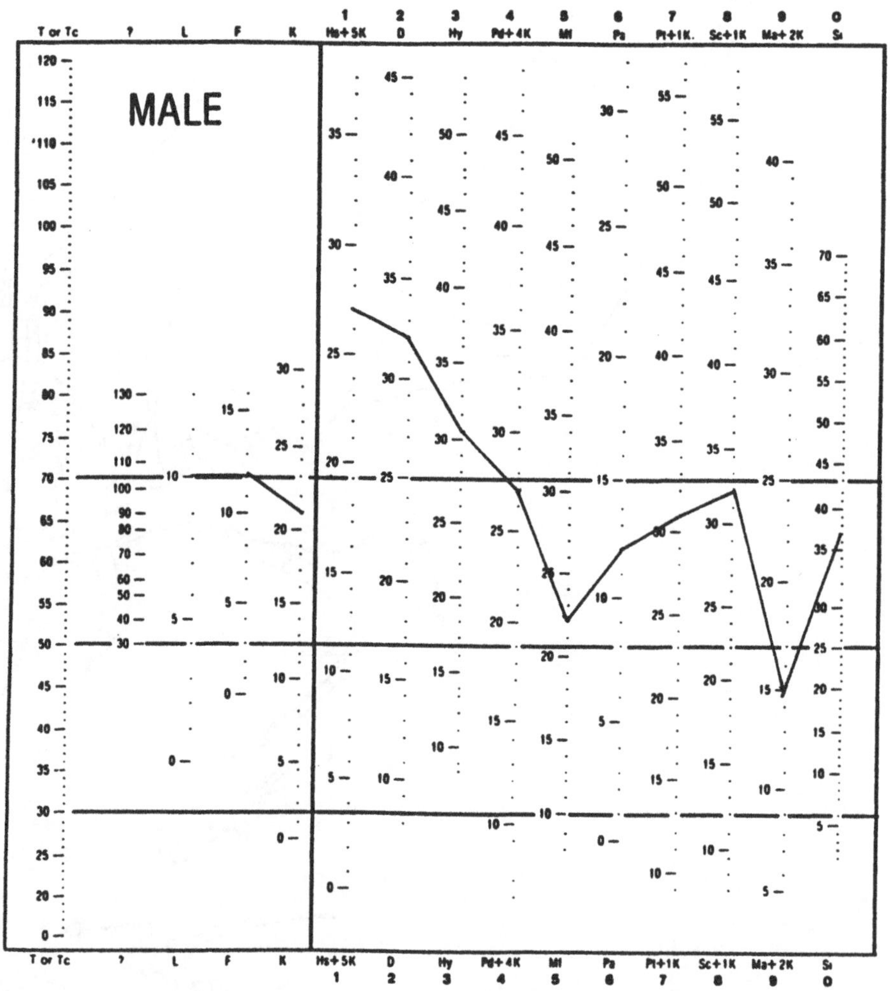

	?	L	F	K	Hs+5K	D	Hy	Pd+4K	Mf	Pa	Pt+1K	Sc+1K	Ma+2K	Si
Raw Score	0	10	12	21	16	32	31	19	22	12	10	11	11	37
K to be added					11			8			21	21	4	
Raw Score with K					27			27			31	32	15	

Figure 5.40A. Male, teen

Figure 5.40B. Male, teen

Figure 5.41. Female, age 12

good student and school cheerleader. Her presenting problem was headaches of a severe and debilitating nature. Her brain scan was negative and medication was ineffective. The issues were eventually determined to reside with the mother, who had suffered from child abuse and was terrified that she might abuse her own children. Work with the mother resulted in the disappearance of the daughter's symptoms. Of course, not all individuals with a tendency to somatisize will oblige by providing a bedridden figure in the drawing.

CONCLUSIONS

As clearly as these drawings appear to exemplify areas of major difficulty in self-concept and relationships with others, the drawings in their entirety simply do not reflect a total, easily recognizable set of consistent representations of pathology that can distinguish them from those of so-called normal individuals. In fact, they represent a clear warning of the cautions to be applied so that the drawings may be viewed as communications of highly individual inner states.

There are many temptations to overinterpret in work with drawings. The reminder must appear here that notions derived from scrutiny of drawings offer only areas for exploration and verification through other procedures.

Each drawing is highly specific and presents an individual story. The story may perhaps be better understood by some knowledge of what might be termed the "language" of drawings, a nonverbal language that seems to use a number of surprisingly consistent ways of communicating feelings, attitudes, and moods. Work with drawings over the years by a number of investigators has yielded a fascinating body of material that certainly may add depth to the understanding of mother-and-child drawings. In these drawings the focus remains on the relationship portrayed between mother and child that seems to set the emotional tone for the sense of self and expectations from the world.

Recommended Readings

Amos, S. P. (1982). The diagnostic, prognostic, and therapeutic implications of schizophrenic art. *Arts in psychotherapy, 9*, 131–143.

Balint, M. (1959). *Thrills and regressions*. New York: International Universities Press.

Case, C. (1990). Reflections and shadows: An exploration of the world of the rejected girl. In C. Case & T. Dalley (Eds.), *Working with children in art therapy*. London: Tavistock/Routledge.

Cavallo, M. A., & Robbins, A. (1980). Understanding an object relations theory through a psychodynamically oriented expressive therapy approach. *Arts in psychotherapy, 7*, 113–123.

Despert, J. L. (1975). *The inner voices of children*. New York: Brunner/Mazel.

Emde, R. N. (Ed.). (1983). *Rene A. Spitz: Dialogues from infancy*. New York: International Universities Press.

Freud, Sophie. (1988). *My three mothers and other passions*. New York: New York University Press.

Gardner, H. (1980). *Artful scribbles*. New York: Basic Books.

Hammer, E. F. (1984). *Creativity, talent and personality*. Malabar, FL: Robert E. Krieger.

Jung, C. G. (1959/1970). Psychological aspects of the mother archetype. In *Four archetypes* (R. F. C. Hull, Trans.). Princeton, NJ: Princeton University Press.

Jung, C. G., von Franz, M.-L., Henderson, J. L., Jacobi, J., & Jaffe, A. (1964). *Man and his symbols*. Garden City, NY: Doubleday.

Kellogg, R. (1970). *Analyzing children's art*. Palo Alto, CA: Mayfield.

Klepsch, M., & Logie, L. (1982). *Children draw and tell: An introduction to the projective uses of children's human figure drawings*. New York: Brunner/Mazel.

Landgarten, H. B. (1981). *Clinical art therapy.* New York: Brunner/Mazel.
Landgarten, H. B., & Lubbers, D. (Eds.). (1991). *Adult art psychotherapy.* New York: Brunner/Mazel.
Lindstrom, M. (1957). *Children's art.* Berkeley: University of California Press.
Masterson, J. F. (1985). *The real self: A developmental, self, and object relations approach.* New York: Brunner/Mazel.
Missildine, W. H. (1983). *Your inner child of the past.* New York: Pocket Books.
Piontelli, A. (1992). *From fetus to child.* London: Tavistock/Routledge.
Rank, O. (1932/1959). Art and artist. In P. Freund (Ed.), C. F. Atkinson (Trans.), *The myth of the birth of the hero* (Sec. I through VII). New York: Vintage.
Rubin, J. A. (1984). *Child art therapy* (2nd ed.). New York: Van Nostrand Reinhold.
Stern, D. N. (1985). *The interpersonal world of the infant.* New York: Basic Books.
Stern, D. N. (1990). *Diary of a baby.* New York: Basic Books.
Winnicott, D. W. (1987). *Babies and their mothers.* Reading, MA: Addison-Wesley.
Winnicott, D.W. (1988). *Human nature.* New York: Schocken Books.

References

Anastasi, A. (1982). *Psychological testing* (5th ed.). New York: Macmillan.

Berne, E. (1961). *Transactional analysis in psychotherapy*. New York: Grove Press.

Bieliauskas, V. J. (1980). *The House-Tree-Person (H-T-P) research review: 1980 edition.* Los Angeles: Western Psychological Services.

Blanck, G., & Blanck, R. (1974). *Ego psychology: Theory and practice*. New York: Columbia University Press.

Bollas, C. (1987). *The shadow of the object: Psychoanalysis of the unthought known.* London: Free Association Books.

Bradshaw. J. (1990). *Homecoming: Reclaiming and championing your inner child.* New York: Bantam.

Buck, J. N. (1948). The H-T-P technique, a qualitative and quantitative scoring manual. *Journal of clinical psychology*, *4*, 317-396.

Buck, J. N. (1966). *The House-Tree-Person technique: Revised manual*. Los Angeles: Western Psychological Services.

Burns, R. C. (1982). *Self-growth in families*. New York: Brunner/Mazel.

Burns, R. C., & Kaufman, S. H. (1970). *Kinetic family drawings (K-F-D)*. New York: Brunner/Mazel.

Burns, R. C. & Kaufman, S. H. (1972). *Actions, styles and symbols in kinetic family drawings*. New York: Brunner/Mazel.

Cressen, R. (1975). Artistic quality of drawings and judges' evaluations of the DAP. *Journal of personality assessment*, *39*(2), 132-137.

Dennis, W. (1966). *Group values through children's drawings*. New York: Wiley.

Di Leo, J. H. (1973). *Children's drawings as diagnostic aids*. New York: Brunner/Mazel.

Dixon, W. J., & Massey, F. J., Jr. (1969). *Introduction to statistical analysis*. New York: McGraw-Hill.

Fairbairn, W. R. D. (1954). *An object-relations theory of the personality*. New York: Basic Books.

Feher, E., Vandecreek, L., & Teglasi, H. (1983). The problem of art quality in the use of human figure drawing tests. *Journal of clinical psychology, 39*(2), 268-275.

Freud, A. (1965). Normality and pathology in childhood. In *The writings of Anna Freud* (Vol. 6). New York: International Universities Press.

Freud, A. (1937/1966). The ego and the mechanisms of defense (rev. ed.). In *The writings of Anna Freud* (Vol. 2). New York: International Universities Press.

Freud, A. (1981). Psychoanalytic psychology of normal development. In *The writings of Anna Freud* (Vol. 8). New York: International Universities Press.

Freud, S. (1958). The Moses of Michelangelo (A. Strachey, Trans.). In B. Nelson (Ed.), *On creativity and the unconscious.* New York: Harper & Row. (Original work published 1914)

Freud, S. (1963). The relation of the poet to day-dreaming (I. F. G. Duff, Trans.). In P. Rieff (Ed.), *Character and culture.* New York: Macmillan. (Original work published 1908)

Fuller, P. (1987). Mother and child in Henry Moore and Winnicott. In J. Fielding & A. Newman (Eds.), *Winnicott studies* (No. 2). London: The Squiggle Foundation.

Gedo, J. E. (1983). *Portraits of the artist.* New York: Guilford.

Gilbert, J. (1978). *Interpreting psychological test data* (Vol. I). New York: Van Nostrand Reinhold.

Gilligan, C. (1982). *In a different voice.* Cambridge, MA: Harvard University Press.

Gilligan, C., Lyons, N. P., & Hanmer, T. J. (Eds.). (1990). *Making connections.* Cambridge, MA: Harvard University Press.

Goodenough, F. L. (1926). *Measurement of intelligence by drawings.* New York: Harcourt, Brace & World.

Guntrip, H. (1971). *Psychoanalytic theory, therapy, and the self.* New York: Basic Books.

Hammer, E. F. (1964). *The House-Tree-Person (H-T-P) clinical research manual.* Los Angeles: Western Psychological Services.

Hammer, E. F. (1986). Graphic techniques with children and adolescents. In A. I. Rabin (Ed.), *Projective techniques for adolescents and children.* New York: Springer.

Harris, D. B. (1963). *Children's drawings as measures of intellectual maturity.* New York: Harcourt Brace Jovanovich.

Harrower, M., Thomas, C. B., & Altman, A. (1975). Human figure drawings in a prospective study of six disorders: Hypertension, coronary heart disease, malignant tumor, suicide, mental illness, and emotional disturbance. *Journal of nervous and mental disease, 161*(3), 191-199.

Hartmann, H. (1964). *Essays on ego psychology.* New York: International Universities Press.

Hedges, L. E. (1983). *Listening perspectives in psychotherapy.* New York: Jason Aronson.

Hedges, L. E. (1992). *Interpreting the countertransference.* New York: Jason Aronson.

Heller, P. (1990). *A child analysis with Anna Freud* (S. Burckhardt & M. Weigand, Trans. Revised by the author.). Madison, CT: International Universities Press.

Jacobson, E. (1964). *The self and the object world.* New York: International Universities Press.
Jolles, I. (1964). *A catalog for the qualitative interpretation of the House-Tree-Person (H-T-P).* Los Angeles: Western Psychological Services.
Kay, S. R. (1978). Qualitative differences in human figure drawings according to schizophrenic subtype. *Perceptual and Motor Skills, 47,* 923-932.
Kellogg, R. (1967). *The psychology of children's art.* New York: CRM-Random House.
Kellogg, R. (1979). *Children's drawings/children's minds.* New York: Grune & Stratton.
Kernberg, O. F. (1975). *Borderline conditions and pathological narcissism.* New York: Jason Aronson.
Klein, M. (1948/1975). *Love, guilt and reparation & other works, 1921-1945.* New York: Delacorte Press.
Koppitz, E. M. (1968). *Psychological evaluation of children's human figure drawings.* New York: Grune & Stratton.
Langer, C. (1992). *Mother and child in art.* New York: Crescent Books.
Lawrence, M. (1975). *Mother and child.* New York: Thomas Y. Crowell.
Machover, K. (1949). *Personality projection in the drawing of the human figure.* Springfield, IL: Charles C Thomas.
Mahler, M. S., Pine, F., & Bergman, A. (1975). *The psychological birth of the human infant.* New York: Basic Books.
Malchiodi, C. (1990). *Breaking the silence.* New York: Brunner/Mazel.
Miljkovitch, M., & Irvine, G. M. (1982). Comparison of drawing performances of schizophrenics, other psychiatric patients and normal schoolchildren on a draw-a-village task. *Arts in psychotherapy, 9,* 203-216.
Miller, J. (1976). *Toward a new psychology of women.* Boston: Beacon Press.
Neumann, E. (1955/1963). *The great mother* (R. Manheim, Trans.). Princeton, NJ: Princeton University Press.
Oster, G. D., & Gould, P. (1987). *Using drawings in assessment and therapy.* New York: Brunner/Mazel.
Reznikoff, M., & Reznikoff, H. R. (1956). The family drawing test: A comparative study of children's drawings. *Journal of clinical psychology, 20,* 467-470.
Rubin, J. A., Ragins, N., Schachter, J., & Wimberly, F. (1979). Drawings by schizophrenic and non-schizophrenic mothers and their children. *Art Psychotherapy, 6,* 163-175.
Sandler, J. (1975). Sexual fantasies and sexual theories in childhood. In *Studies in child psychoanalysis: Pure and applied.* (Monograph Series of the Psychoanalytic Study of the Child, No. 5). New Haven: Yale University Press.
Sandler, J., with Freud, A. (1985). *The analysis of defense: The ego and the mechanisms of defense revisited.* New York: International Universities Press.
Schaverien, J. (1992). *The revealing image.* London: Tavistock/Routledge.
Schildkrout, M. D., Shenker, I. R., & Sonnenblick, M. (1972). *Human figure drawings in adolescence.* New York: Brunner/Mazel.
Schneider, D. E. (1950/1962). *The psychoanalyst and the artist.* New York: Mentor.
Shaffer, J. W., Duszynski, K. R., & Thomas, C. B. (1984). A comparison of three methods for scoring figure drawings. *Journal of personality assessment, 48*(3), 245-254.

Silverman, L. H., Lachmann, F. M., & Milich, R. H. (1982). *The search for oneness*. New York: International Universities Press.

Silverman, L. H., Lachmann, F. M., & Milich, R. H. (1984). Unconscious oneness fantasies: Experimental findings and implications for treatment. *International forum for psychoanalysis*, *1*(2), 107-152.

Silverman, L. H., & Weinberger, J. (1985). Mommy and I are one. *American psychologist*, *40*(12), 1296-1308.

Simon, R. (1988). Marion Milner and the psychotherapy of art. In J. Fielding & A. Newman (Eds.), *Winnicott studies* (No. 3). London: Squiggle Foundation.

Simon, R. M. (1992). *The symbolism of style*. London: Tavistock/Routledge.

Sims, J., Dana, R. H., & Bolton, B. (1983). The validity of the Draw-A-Person Test as an anxiety measure. *Journal of personality assessment*, *47*(3), 250-257.

Spielberger, C. D., Gorsuch, R. L., & Lushene, R. E. (1970). *STAI manual for the State-Trait Anxiety Inventory*. Palo Alto, CA: Consulting Psychologists Press.

Spitz, R. (1965). *The first year of life*. New York: International Universities Press.

Sullivan, H. S. (1953). *The interpersonal theory of psychiatry*. New York: W. W. Norton.

Tobey, S. (1991). *Art of motherhood*. New York: Abbeville Press.

Wenck, L. S. (1977). *House-Tree-Person drawings: An illustrated diagnostic handbook*. Los Angeles: Western Psychological Services.

Winnicott, D. W. (1965). Ego distortions in terms of true and false self. In *Maturational processes and the facilitating environment*. New York: International Universities Press.

Winnicott, D. W. (1971/1980). *Playing and reality*. Harmondsworth, Middlesex, England: Penguin.

Wood, J. (1992). *The nativity*. London: Scala Publications.

Wysocki, A. C., & Wysocki, B. A. (1977). Human figure drawings of sex offenders. *Journal of clinical psychology*, *33*(1), 278-284.

Index